YOGA
THE BODY MIND & THE DIVINE

Govindji
Salim Pushpanath

Presented by:

Kerala - India
www.sreesankara.com

Yoga

The Body, Mind & the Divine

Yoga

The Body, Mind & the Divine

By : Govindji

Photography & Concept: Salim Pushpanath

Design: Dinkar
Production Co-ordinator: Thomas Kurian
Colour management by: Brijilal
Reproduction by: www.colortone.co.in

Printed and bound by Times Offset (M) Sdn Bhd, Malaysia

ISBN 81-88000-16-7

Published by Salim Pushpanath
DEE BEE INFO PUBLICATIONS
"Pushpanath" Malloossery, Kottayam - 686 041. Kerala, India.
Tel: 00 481 2391429, 2302799.
www.dbventure.com
Email: salimpushpanath@gmail.com

Printed in Malyasia

Yoga

The Body, Mind & the Divine...

In Perfect Accord

Yoga is a physiological, psychosomatic and sacred order practiced by the Yogis of ancient India that advocates a way-of-life seamlessly and in perfect accord with oneself and his/her environment. Derived from Sanskrit Yoga translates to mean harmony in unity. Yoga is a complete life science and is the oldest system of personal development in the world encompassing the entire body, mind and spirit. It is the union between a person's own consciousness and the universal consciousness.

The ancient yogis had a profound understanding of man's essential nature and of what he needs to live in harmony with himself and his environment. They perceived the physical self as a means of transport, with the mind as the driver, the soul as man's true identity, and action, emotion and intelligence as the three forces that sustain it efficiently. These forces must be in perfect balance and integrate flawlessly for the right functioning of a human being. Considering the fine relationship between body and mind, the Yogis formulated a unique method for maintaining this balance - a method that combines all the movements you need for physical health in combination with breathing and meditation techniques that ensure peace of mind.

The classical techniques of Yoga date back more than 5,000 years. In ancient times, the desire for greater personal freedom, health and long life, and heightened self-understanding gave birth to this system of physical and mental exercise that has since become so popular world-wide. Yoga is a method of learning that aims to attain the unity of mind, body, and spirit through these three main Yoga structures: exercise, breathing, and meditation. The exercises of Yoga are designed to put pressure on the glandular systems of the body, thereby

increasing its efficiency and total health. The body is looked upon as the primary instrument that enables us to work and evolve in the world, a Yoga student; therefore, treats it with great care and respect. The Breathing Techniques are based on the concept that breath is the source of life in the body.

Yoga practitioners gently increase their breath control to improve the health and the function of both body and mind. These two systems prepare the body and mind for meditation, making it easier for students to achieve a quiet mind and be free from everyday stress. Regular daily practice of all three parts of this structure of Yoga results in a clear, bright mind and a strong, capable body.

The science of Yoga is vast and divided into many branches and each branch focuses on attaining union with the Divine or the greatness of human potential. The main branches of Yoga are as follows: Hatha Yoga advocates mastery of breath and body and is the most well known Yoga especially in the Western world. Raja Yoga works through the mastery of the mind by mastering consciousness and stilling of the mind. Jnana Yoga works through the understanding the self and involves the study of your preferred scriptures and meditation. Bhakthi Yoga works through love and devotion and involves a preferred deity or guru and expression of total devotion through rites, rituals, singing and praising. Karma Yoga works through selflessness and service. Mantra Yoga works through mental or vocal repetition of sacred words. Kundalini or Laya Yoga works through the awakening of latent psychic forces through several energy centres or charkas involving intense meditation and breath suspension practices. Tantric Yoga works through harnessing of sexual energy and prepares one for the union of male and female in order to achieve union with the Divine.

The focus of this book is on Hatha Yoga but also involves some components of Raja Yoga as an introduction to meditation.

Keeping equilibrium in all activities, such as eating, walking, all kinds of work, sleeping etc, is Yoga which destroys all kinds of sorrows.

HATHA YOGA

Hatha is a compound term that means the sun and the moon. This is a reference to the balance between yin and yang, hot and cold, male and female including all opposites that are balancing pairs. When people mention the term Yoga, they usually refer to Hatha Yoga. Hatha Yoga is the most popular branch of Yoga and from which a lot of the styles of Yoga originated. Hatha Yogis consider the body as the vehicle for the soul. They use physical postures or Asanas, Breathing Techniques or Pranayama, and Meditation in order to achieve ideal bodily health so that the subtle spiritual elements of the mind emerge freely.

Hatha Yoga is often translated as the branch of Yoga that brings union of the pairs of opposites referring to the positive (sun) and negative (moon) currents in the system. In Yoga the flow of breath through the right nostril is called sun breath and the flow through the left nostril is called moon breath. Hatha Yoga concentrates on the third (Asana) and fourth (Pranayama) steps in the Eight Limbs of Yoga. It uses the physical postures and breathing techniques in order to energise and clear the energy channels called the Nadis, removing the obstacles for the other Limbs - Pratyahara, Dharana, Dhyana and Samadhi. Asanas are designed to improve health and bring energy to the body and mind that is necessary in opening the Nadis. It can also serve as a meditation posture, which can make you feel perfectly comfortable for a longer period of time. Mastering the Asanas can help develop your will power, concentration and self-withdrawal or not bothering too much about the input of the senses. These Asana benefits directly open the path to Prathyahara and Dharana.

Pranayamas, on the other hand, is highly vital in the practice of Hatha Yoga. One needs to master his breathing patterns before he can master his mind Pranayamas regulate the flow of Prana or vital energy in the body that is needed to take further steps toward Samadhi. The practice of Pranayama can also lead to the awakening of the Kundalini Energy. Practising Hatha Yoga can help you recognise the divine halo within you. It can also help you become stronger, more flexible and relaxed. The relaxation exercises involved in practising Hatha Yoga opens the energy channels allowing your spiritual energy to flow freely. `Certain Asanas also massages and tones internal organs, which facilitates in the prevention, management and treatment of certain ailments such as diabetes, arthritis and hypertension. Breathing Exercises can also help patients of asthma and Bronchitis. Hatha Yoga practice is also a great way to cope with stress, relieve tension and rid oneself of anxiety and depression.

The Benefits of Yoga

Yoga and health are two words that are very closely related. The health benefits of Yoga are widely known and acknowledged. Yoga is a popular aid in improving and attaining both physical and mental health. This is basically the most common reason why people practice Yoga - for optimum health. They want to ease their back pain, find a method to ease stress, or ways to deal with their well being

"The Yogi regards the physical body as an instrument for his journey toward perfection." Swami Vishnu-Devananda. Yoga is a science of health - unlike modern medicine, which is largely a science of disease and treatment. The teachings of Yoga are based on intricate and precise understanding of the healthy functioning of the human body and mind. Its techniques are designed to maximise your own potential for good health, vitality and lasting youthfulness. This section describes the functioning of our body, looking in particular at the three major functions: the body's strong, flexible frame of muscles, bones and ligaments; the nutrient cycles of digestion, respiration and circulation which nourishes every cell and tissue; and the vital messenger systems of nerves and hormones which balance and regulate our physical, emotional and mental responses.

Yoga aims to unite the mind, the body, and the spirit. Yogis view that the mind and the body as one, and that if it is given the right tools and taken to the right environment, it can find harmony and heal itself. Yoga is considered therapeutic. It helps you to become more aware of your body's posture, alignment and patterns of movement. It makes the body more flexible and helps you relax even in the midst of a stressful environment.

This is one of the foremost reasons why people want to start practising yoga - to feel fitter, be more energetic and be happier and content.

Yoga is a science that has been practised for thousands of years. It consists of ancient theories, observations and principles about the mind and body connection which is now being proven by modern medicine. Substantial research has been conducted to look at the health benefits of Yoga - from the Yoga postures (Asanas), Yoga breathing (Pranayama) and Meditation. The information is grouped into three categories-physiological, psychological, biochemical effects. Furthermore, scientists have laid these results against the benefits of regular exercise.

Physiological Benefits

- Stable autonomic nervous system equilibrium
- Pulse rate decreases
- Blood Pressure decreases (of special significance for hypo reactors)
- Galvanic Skin Response (GSR) increases
- EEG - alpha waves increase (theta, delta, and beta waves also increase during various stages of meditation)
- EMG activity decreases
- Cardiovascular efficiency increases
- Respiratory efficiency increases
- Gastrointestinal function normalises
- Endocrine function normalises
- Excretory functions improve
- Musculoskeletal flexibility and joint range of motion increase
- Breath-holding time increases
- Joint range of motion increase
- Grip strength increases
- Eye-hand co-ordination improves
- Dexterity skills improve
- Reaction time improves
- Posture improves
- Strength and resiliency increase
- Endurance increases
- Energy level increases
- Weight normalises
- Sleep improves
- Immunity increases
- Pain decreases
- Steadiness improves
- Depth perception improves
- Balance improves
- Integrated functioning of body parts improves

Psychological Benefits

- Somatic and kinaesthetic awareness increase
- Mood improves and subjective well-being increases
- Self-acceptance and self-actualisation increase
- Social adjustment increases
- Anxiety and depression decrease
- Hostility decreases
- Concentration improves
- Attention improves
- Mood improves
- Self-actualisation increase
- Social skills increases
- Well-being increases
- Somatic and kinaesthetic awareness increase
- Self-acceptance increase
- Attention improves
- Concentration improves
- Memory improves
- Learning efficiency improves
- Symbol coding improves
- Depth perception improves
- Flicker fusion frequency improves

Biochemical Benefits

- Glucose decreases
- Sodium decreases
- Total cholesterol decreases
- Triglycerides decrease
- HDL cholesterol increases
- LDL cholesterol decreases
- Cholinesterase increases
- Catecholamines decrease
- ATPase increases
- Hematocrit increases
- Haemoglobin increases
- Lymphocyte count increases

"Synchronizing mind and body is not a concept or a random
technique someone thought up for self-improvement. Rather,
it is a basic principle of how to be a human being and how to use
your sense perceptions, your mind and your body together."

- Total white blood cell count decreases
- Thyroxin increases
- Vitamin C increases
- Total serum protein increases

Advantages of Yoga...

- Parasympathetic nervous system dominates
- Sub cortical regions of brain dominate
- Slow dynamic and static movements
- Normalisation of muscle tone
- Low risk of injuring muscles and ligaments
- Low caloric consumption
- Effort is minimised, relaxed
- Energising (breathing is natural or controlled)
- Balanced activity of opposing muscle groups
- Non-competitive, process oriented
- Awareness is internal (focus is on breath and
- the infinite)
- Limitless possibilities for growth in self-awareness

Versus Regular Exercise.

- Sympathetic Nervous System dominates
- Cortical regions of brain dominate
- Rapid forceful movements
- Increased muscle tension
- Higher risk of injury
- Moderate to high caloric consumption
- Effort is maximised
- Fatiguing (breathing is taxed)
- Imbalance activity of opposing groups
- Competitive, goal-oriented
- Awareness is external (focus is on reaching the toes, reaching the finish line, etc.)
- Boredom factor

A history of Yoga

Though Yoga's Origin is shrouded, evidence links the earliest Yoga tradition back at least 5000 years to the beginning of human civilisation. Scholars believe that Yoga grew out of Stone Age Shamanism, because of the cultural similarities between Modern Hinduism and Mehrgarh, a Neolithic settlement. In fact, much of Hindu ideas, rituals and symbols of today appear to have their roots in this shamanistic culture of Mehrgarh. Early Yoga and archaic shamanism had much in common as both sought to transcend the human condition. The primary goal of shamanism was to heal members of the community and act as religious mediators.

Archaic Yoga was also community oriented, as it attempted to discern the cosmic order through inner vision, then to apply that order to daily living. Later, Yoga evolved into a more inward experience, and Yogis focused on their individual enlightenment and salvation. The first archaeological evidence of Yoga's existence is found in stone seals excavated from the Indus valley. The stone seals depict figures performing Yoga postures.

The Indus was the largest and most advanced civilisation in the ancient world and exceptionally modern for its time. Indus was a maritime society, exporting goods throughout the Middle East and Africa. They constructed multi-storey buildings, a sewage system, and laid out geometrical brick roads.

The Vedas

The Indus civilisation also gave birth to the ancient texts known as the Vedas, the oldest scriptures in the world. The Vedas is a collection of hymns that praises a higher power; it contains the oldest recorded Yogic teachings and is considered divine revelation. Thus, the wisdom of the Vedas is known as Vedic or Pre-classical Yoga. Vedic Yoga is characterised by ritualistic ceremonies from which the Yoga practice that requires Yoga practitioners to transcend the limitations of the mind originated.

Vedic literature is replete with references to prayerful contemplation; (Brahman), higher vision; (dhi), and; the ideal harmony; (rita). Vedic people relied on rishis (dedicated Vedic Yogis) to teach them how to live in Divine harmony. Through intensive spiritual practice, rishis were often gifted with visions of the ultimate reality. Later texts known as the Brahmanas were written to explain the rituals and hymns of the Vedas. The Aranyakas texts followed, detailing rituals for Yogis living in the seclusion of the forest. This era also served as the beginning of India's medical tradition known as Ayurveda.

Pre-classical Yoga

Sometime between 1800 and 1500 B.C., Gnostic texts called the Upanishads appeared. The 200 or so scriptures comprising the Upanishads explained the transcendental self; (atman) and its relation to the ultimate reality (Brahman). The Karma doctrine is believed to have originated with the Upanishads as well. Just as the New Testament rests upon and furthers the Old Testament, so too, the Upanishads further expounds upon the scriptures of the Vedas. The teaching of the Upanishads dawned the era of Pre-classical Yoga.

Around 1400 B.C., the renowned sage Vyasa, categorised the Vedic hymns into the 4 Vedic texts as we know today: Rig-Veda ("KnowledgeofPraise"), Yajur-Veda ("Knowledge of Sacrifice"), Sama-Veda ("Knowledge of Chants"), and Atharva-Veda ("Knowledge of Atharvan"). In 1200 B.C., an enlightened teacher Rishabha started the tradition known as Jainism, which is also dedicated to the liberation of the spirit. Then in 1000 B.C., a second urbanisation began along the Gangetic plains. Later, in the sixth century B.C., Lord Buddha spread the teaching of Buddhism, which stresses the importance of meditation and ethics over physical postures. Buddhism had some similarities with Hinduism; however, Yoga sages saw the limitations of ignoring the physical purification process. Siddhartha Gautama Buddha was skilled in meditation and Yoga, attained enlightenment at the age of 35.

Today The Bhagavad-Gita has had perhaps, the most profound influence on Hindu culture and philosophy. This ancient text was written about 500 B.C. and is the first scripture devoted entirely to Yoga. The Bhagavad-Gita confirms that Yoga was quite ancient by the time of its writing. Only 700 verses long, The Gita is a conversation between Prince Arjuna and the Lord Krishna. The Gita's message is to oppose evil in the world. The Gita earned its relevance because of its attempt to blend Jnana Yoga, Bhakati Yoga and Karma Yoga together unifying these various Yogic traditions. Gita also deals with Raja Yoga, Dhyana Yoga and Sanyasa Yoga (Yoga of renunciation). Many schools during this era taught ways of attaining heightened levels of meditation in order to surpass the mind and body to achieve one's self.

Buddhism quickly grew, and in 480 B.C. senior disciples of Buddha systematised the Buddhist teachings. For the next few hundred years, the canonical scriptures of Buddhism were structured. In 300 B.C., Jaimini composed the Mimamsa-Sutra, the first authoritative text of Hinduism. Jaimini is regarded as a disciple of Vyasa. Soon after this, Emperor Ashoka converted to Buddhism and extensively spread Buddhism. This was the greatest era of Buddhist influence in India.

Classical Yoga

After the turn of the millennium, the spread of Yoga in its different forms gave rise to the need for standardisation. Thus in the second century B.C., Patanjali composed a seminal text, Yoga-Sutra and defined Classical Yoga. The 195 aphorisms or sutras that comprise the Yoga Sutra, expound upon Raja-Yoga (the eightfold Yoga path). The Yoga Sutra was intended to be memorised as a means of internalising its wisdom. The Eight Limbs of Classical Yoga are: 1) yama, or restraint, 2) niyama, or observance of purity, tolerance and study, 3) Asana, or Physical Exercises, 4) Pranayama or control of breath energy, 5) pratyahara, or controlling the outer senses, 6) dharana, or concentration, 7) dhyana or meditation and 8) samadhi or absorption in the sublime. Patanjali advocates studying the sacred scriptures as part of the Yoga practice, which becomes Classical Yoga's distinct feature.

The real ground breaking characteristic of Yoga-Sutra however, is its precept of philosophical dualism. Patanjali believed that separation of the matter (prakriti) and spirit (purusha) were necessary to cleanse the spirit to absolute purity. This is in stark contrast to Pre-classical and Vedic Yoga, which adopts the unification of the body and the spirit. The teachings of Patanjali represent a departure from traditional non-dualistic Yoga and laid the groundwork for Postclassical Yoga. For centuries after Patanjali, the dualism of Yoga was predominant. Yogis focused almost exclusively on meditation and neglected the Asanas. They were attempting to exit the mortal coil and merge with the ultimate reality through contemplation. But with the advent of alchemy, a precursor to chemistry, the Yoga masters rekindled their belief in the body as a temple. Contemporary thought shifted to health, longevity and maintenance. As such, the Yoga masters attempted to demonstrate that new Yoga techniques fundamentally alters the body's biochemistry and makes it immortal. This led back to the Pre-classical and Vedic Yoga belief about the primacy of the Asana and to the beginning of Postclassical Yoga.

Post-Classical Yoga

The era of Postclassical Yoga gave rise to prolific literature, the different branches of Yoga that includes the Hatha and the Tantra, and to many holistic schools for Yoga. Postclassical Yoga can best be defined as an appreciation of the present moment. Practitioners no longer aspired to liberation from this reality, rather to accept it and live at the moment. Modern Yoga arrived during the late 1800s. It can be attributed to many gurus, including Swami Vivekananda, and their apostolic works.

Another Yoga guru, who is perhaps the most popular, was Swami Paramashansa Yogananda, who founded the Self-Realisation Fellowship. Yogananda wrote Autobiography of a Yogi and his teachings still enjoy immense popularity even today. Other Yoga gurus include Krishnamurti and Maharishi Mahesh Yogi. Krishnamurti travelled widely, drawing large crowds and expounded upon Jnana-Yoga. People will most likely remember Maharishi Mahesh Yogi who popularised Transcendental Meditation (TM) in the 60's, because he was associated with the Beatles.

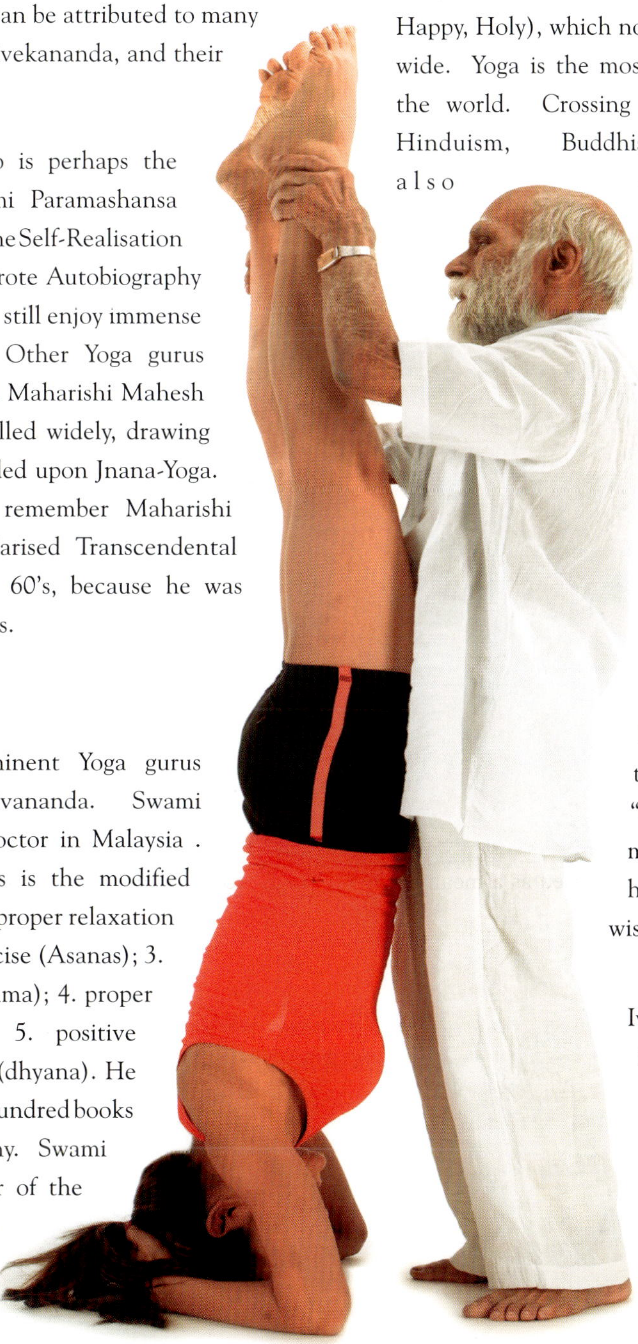

Yoga Today

One of the most prominent Yoga gurus is Himalayan Swami Sivananda. Swami Sivananda served as a doctor in Malaysia . Among Sivanand's works is the modified Five Principles of Yoga: 1. proper relaxation (savasana); 2. proper exercise (Asanas); 3. proper breathing (pranayama); 4. proper diet (vegetarian), and; 5. positive thinking and Meditation (dhyana). He also wrote more than two hundred books about Yoga and Philosophy. Swami Sivananda is the founder of the International Sivananda Yoga Vedanta Centres through his disciple, Swami Vishnu-devananada. Swami Vishnu-devananada also wrote the Illustrated book of Yoga.

Swami Sivananda's other notable disciples include: Swami Satchitananda who introduced chanting and Yoga to Wood-stock; Swami Sivananada Radha, the woman who explored the connection between psychology and Yoga, and; Yogi Bhajan who started teaching Kundalini Yoga in the 70s. He also founded the 3HO organisation (Healthy, Happy, Holy), which now has around 200 centres world-wide. Yoga is the most diversified spiritual practice in the world. Crossing over many cultures (including Hinduism, Buddhism, Jainism and the West), Yoga also extends over multiple languages. The Yogic tradition continues to proliferate and spread its message of peace to this very day.

Yogacharya B.K.S. Iyengar with his intellectual and spiritual practices has masterminded the techniques which can be used by all practitioners of yoga. "Research based experience" and "experience based research" has helped him in evolving this technique which is now known as "Iyengar Yoga". He has therefore made it possible for ordinary human beings to experience the wisdom of the yoga sutras.

Iyengar yoga is meant for all and is a way of life. The use of props, designed by Guruji , such as wooden gadgets, belts, ropes helps the practitioner to achieve perfection in any asana. Regular practice of 'Iyengar Yoga' definitely integrates the body, mind and emotions.

Adore the great sage Patanjali who protects chitta
(mind stuff) by yoga, the language by grammar and purifies
the body by treatment.

The Aim of Yoga

The aim of Yoga is to attain perfection of the intellect both of the head and the heart so that the practitioner is devoted, true and pure. This demands an almost total abandonment of other interests other than in this path. The mind is in a state of constant fluidity and chases sensual pleasures. According to Patanjali the mind must be controlled and then sublimated to achieve perfection in Yoga.

Yoga requires acute sharpness of intellect and alert organs of perception. There is no competition in Yoga but it requires freedom to think and reconstruct with a desire to perform better. This brings the Yogi his/her most exalted enlightenment and wherever the Yogi is or whatever the Yogi does his/her thoughts will constantly be in spiritual communion taking the Yogi to the zenith of spirituality and contentment.

Yoga as an art

According to Dr. S. Radhakrishnan, Yoga is an art of opening the unconscious parts of our being that enables us to feel the magnificence of cosmic conscience. Yoga is an art in all aspects. It is a spiritual art in that it transforms the Yogi and brings him/her in contact with the innermost soul. It is a fine art since it is aesthetic, expressive, representative and imitative. It is a visual art as the body is made to form graceful designs that are stunningly beautiful. It is a very beneficial art for the yogi and is presented as a performing art form for the viewer. The art of Yoga is creative, rhythmic in practice and individualistic in form.

Yoga as a Philosophy

Yoga is a philosophy in that it is a constant search for truth and enlightenment. It is a way of thinking and mental training that helps one to live a pure and noble life. The Yogi is aware that all that exists is a manifestation of Divinity and that Divinity pervades all creations. As everything both the living and the dead manifests consciences in varying degrees and in different stages of evolution. The Yogi strives to reach the root of philosophy that leads to perfection and shows the way to liberation. Yoga is a philosophy leading to the culmination of all knowledge the art of self-realisation. Once a Yogi reaches the frontiers of self-realised knowledge the Yogi merges with the infinite discards the robe of individuality and becomes universal.

Yoga as a Spiritual Experience

Yoga belongs to the field of emotions, instincts, intuitions and insights. It is guided by the principles that are brought to the surface by practices and experiences such that analytical knowledge and factual knowledge are perfectly synchronised. It is a spiritual journey that refines man elevating him/her to a pedestal and filled with elegance and grace. Yoga is a psycho-spiritual experience connecting man with the object of contemplation. The Yogi controls and blends the movements of the body integrating it with his/her consciousness seamlessly moving towards the Supreme. The Yogi refines his/her body and blends the subtle forces of this instrument with reverential devotion and uninterrupted practice as an offering to the Divine. The Yogi chisels his/her body with Asanas, develops the sense by ethics, stores energy through breath tones the consciousness with the brilliance of the inner cosmic rays becoming one with his/her self and thus the body becomes the Yogi's Heaven on Earth

Yoga as a Science

Yoga like all art forms is a science as well as a philosophy. As Yoga analyses the turbulent mind and shows ways and means of achieving the ultimate goal of freedom and oneness with the Universe it is a science. As a science Yoga conveys truth. On a practical level Yoga keeps one's body healthy, the mind calm and sharp, and the self in an elevated state of consciousness. It is therefore a darsana or vision, seeing, acting, showing, exhibiting, teaching, as an aspect or semblance, a doctrine, a system of scientific philosophy. The practical aspect of Yoga conveys the artistic aspect of Yoga with all it's precision and grace.

The Principles of Yoga

The Five Principles of Yoga are the basis of attaining a healthy body and mind through the practice of Yoga. In this section, we give you detailed information on these five principles:

Proper Relaxation

By releasing the tension in the muscles and putting the whole body at rest, you revitalise your nervous system and achieve inner peace, making you feel relaxed and refreshed. This relaxed feeling is carried over into all your activities and helps you conserve your energy and let go of all worries and fears.

Proper Exercise

This principle revolves around the idea that our physical body is meant to move and exercise. Proper Exercise is achieved through the Yoga postures or Asana, which systematically works on all parts of the body - stretches and tones the muscles and Ligaments, enhances the flexibility of the spine and the joints, and improves blood circulation. The Asanas are designed to regulate the physical and physiological functions of the body. Practising these Yoga Postures makes your body relaxed, gives you more strength and energy, and rejuvenates the various systems of the body. The Yoga Posture goes together with proper breathing. Every movement and stretch should be guided by your breath and perfect synchrony. The execution of the Asana is beneficial to the body, and at the same time contributes to spiritual and mental growth.

Proper Breathing

This means breathing fully and rhythmically, making use of all the parts of your lungs to increase your oxygen intake. Proper Breathing should be deep, slow and rhythmical. To achieve this, you need to be able to regulate the length and duration of your inhalation, exhalation, and the retention of air in your lungs or the pauses between breaths. Yogic Breathing Exercises (Pranayama) teaches you how you can recharge your body and control your mental state by regulating the flow of Prana - the life energy. This helps you achieve a calmer and more focused mind, and increases your energy level.

Proper Diet

What you eat extremely affects your mind. Improper diet results to mental inefficiency and blocks spiritual awareness. Proper Diet is one that nourishes both mind and body. It should be well balanced and based on natural foods. Proper Diet in Yoga also means eating in moderation and eating only when you are hungry. We sometimes tend to eat when we are upset, using food to fill the gap or the emptiness that we feel. Bad eating habits will cause our senses to be dull that we won't even notice how much we eat or how it tastes and may result to diet related ailments like obesity and diabetes. Food should sustain our body. It should keep the body light and supple, the mind calm, and it should also help in keeping a strong immune system.

Positive Thinking and Meditation

The way we think highly affects our way of life. Practice keeping a positive outlook in life, this will facilitate in having a peaceful mind. Positive thinking and Meditation helps you remove negative thoughts and retain perfect thought-control.

“The foods that are bitter, sour, saline, excessively hot,
pungent, dry and burning, are liked by the rajasic and are productive
of pain, grief, and disease.” - BHAGAVAD GITA, 17-9

The Six Essential part of Yoga

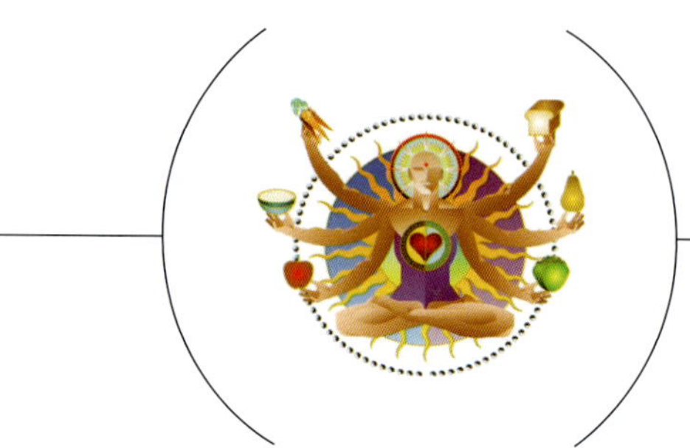

1. Posture *The posture becomes perfect when the effort of achieving it vanishes.*

The practice of Yoga Exercises means practising both your body and your mind towards the Almighty. It takes willpower and perseverance to accomplish each Yoga posture and to practice it daily. But the prize for your perseverance is really worth all the hard work. The practice of Yoga exercises or Asanas can improve your health, increase your resistance, and develop your mental awareness. Doing the Yoga postures requires you to study each posture and execute them slowly as you control your body and your mind.

Yoga Exercises are also known as Asanas, Yoga Postures. These exercises work on all the various system of the body. It makes the spine and joints supple and tone the muscles, glands and internal organs. Though the Asanas may just seem to be merely physical exercises, you will later realise that it is more than exercising your body. As you progress, you will become more aware of the flow of Prana, the vital energy, and the importance of correct breathing - that is creating a union between your breath and your movement.

①

②

2. Breathing *"When the Breath wanders, the mind is unsteady, but when the Breath is still, so is the mind still." Hatha Yoga Pradipika*

Breathing is life. It is one of our most vital functions of Pranayama or controlling the vital energy promotes proper breathing. Proper Breathing, in a Yogic point of view, is to bring more oxygen to the blood and to the brain, and to control prana or the vital life energy. Pranayama - the science of breath control, consists a series of exercises intended to meet these needs and to keep the body in vibrant health.

Pranayama also goes hand in hand with the Asanas. The union of these two Yogic Principles is considered as the highest form of purification and self-discipline, covering both mind and body. Breathing exercises helps you to achieve a calm and alert mind. Some Breathing Exercises also help in removing excess mucus in the body thus help you manage respiratory ailments like asthma and bronchitis.

③

3.Relaxation *"The soul that moves in the world of the senses and yet keeps the senses in harmony... finds rest in quietness." Bhagavad Gita*

In this section, we present the technique of relaxation, that is an essential part of yoga practice. There are three parts to proper relaxation - physical, mental and spiritual relaxation. To relax the body, you lie down in the Corpse Posture and first tense then relax each part of the body in turn, working from up your feet to your head. This alternate tensing then relaxing is necessary because it is only by knowing how tension feels that you can be sure that you have achieved relaxation. Then just as in normal life your mind instructs the muscles to tense and contract, you now use autosuggestion to send the muscles a message to relax. With practice you will gradually learn to use your subconscious mind to extend this control to the involuntary muscles of the heart, the digestive systems and other organs too.

4. Meditation

Meditation is one of the five principles of Yoga. It is the practice by which there is constant observation of the mind. It requires you to focus your mind at one point and stilling the mind in order to perceive the self. Through the practice of Meditation you will achieve a greater sense of purpose and strength of will. It also helps you achieve a clearer mind, improve your concentration, and discover the wisdom and tranquillity within you. Meditation is also one of the eight limbs of Yoga, which leads to samadhi or enlightenment. Research shows that the practice of meditation contributes to our physical and psychological well being. It can reduce blood pressure and relieve stress and pain. Meditating also brings our mind to a level of consciousness that promotes healing or what is known as the alpha state. Achieving the alpha state can help decrease anxiety, depression and other mental, psychological, or emotional problems.

④

"Though no one can go back and make a brand new start,
Anyone can start from now and make a brand new ending."

-CARL BARD

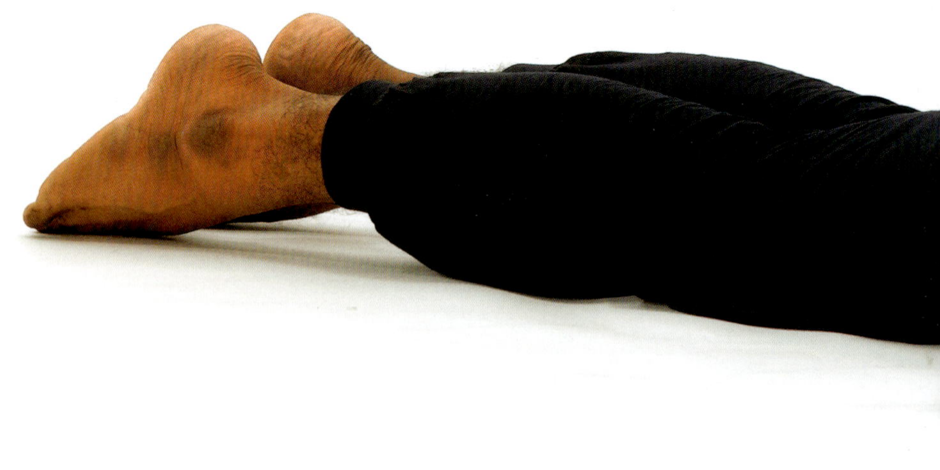

5. Diet *"Let the Yogi eat moderately and abstemiously; otherwise, however clever, he cannot gain success." Siva Samhita.*

Your mind and body is greatly affected by the food that you eat. An improper diet results in mental insufficiency, weak body and blocks spiritual awareness. One of the five principles of Yoga is proper diet. According to this principle, your diet should nourish both mind and body, and should be well balanced and based on natural foods. It also means eating in moderation and eating only when you are hungry.

Yoga Diet is a perfect complement to Yoga practice. Eating properly not only promotes good health but also helps you achieve proper and clearer feelings. Yoga Diet also helps you to balance your weight, that is loose excess weight and maintain a fitter body since it eliminates junk foods from your food list and include only the healthy ones.

Yoga Diet is a pure or "sattvic" diet. It is based on fresh, light and natural food such as fruits, grains and vegetables. It keeps the body lean and supple, and the mind clear and sharp, which is suitable for the practice of Yoga and necessary in everyday life. It also helps prevent health issues like diabetes and obesity etc. Even if you do not intend to become vegetarian, we fully recommend everyone follow these basic diet rules as it will make you feel better and be healthier.

6. Right Thinking: To attain the most out of Yoga requires certain awareness and caring needs to filter through all aspects of life. Yoga is concerned with all aspects that bring about health and vitality of body, mind and spirit. How we think, speak, react and act is all-important and can restrain or accelerate our progress in Yoga. One should aim to be caring towards others by not harming any living creature through thought, word or actions. Through our personal caring and radiance that results from our caring for others we not only improve the quality of our lives but also influence the lives of all whom we meet. Yoga attributes to the principle of Ahimsa or non-violence (unconditional love), Satya or truthfulness, Asatya or stealing, Brahmacharya or controlling the sexual urge (celibacy) and Aparigraha or non-covetousness.

Practising Yoga at Home

Preparation: If you plan to practice Yoga at home it is advisable to join a local Yoga class for additional guidance to this book Moreover a classroom atmosphere can be fun and a teacher would be able to help you achieve the right postures more effectively. You can practice Yoga almost anywhere inside or outside the house with enough space to stretch your limbs. You basically do not need anything to practice Yoga. The important thing is the attitude - a big heart minus ego. Some loose fitting clothes or no clothes at all, and a secluded spot in your house will be enough for you to start with. A balanced diet (sattwik) also aids a great deal in Yoga practice. A four-hour interval between meals is advised. Practising Yoga on a mat or a blanket and a pillow is recommended if and when necessary. Wear a stretch suit or something similar.

It would be ideal to practice Yoga everyday especially in the morning. Remember it is vital that you enjoy your practice and it should not be imposed on you as a strict regiment. Be gentle and calm. Pay attention to how you feel each day and adjust your practice accordingly.

Ideally Yoga should be done each day at the same time as consistency helps encourage discipline and offers the most rewards. The best time is either early mornings or early evenings on an empty stomach. Those who do not find time in the morning can do in the evening before sunset.

The duration of each practice can be anything from 30-minutes to two hours according to your convenience. However it is very important to allow time for postures and relaxation. Never rush your practice if you are having shorter sessions choose only necessary postures. To get the best results it is advisable to set aside at least 60 to 90 minutes for each session. For example: 5-minute warming-up, 40 minutes postures; 5-10 minute relaxation, 5-10 minutes for Pranayama and 5-30 minute meditation. Of course you can juggle your timing as you please.

Working with a partner can be real fun. Partners assist in checking to see the postures are correct and also check for undue strain if any. They can also support you when attempting tricky new postures. It is also safer to work with someone more experienced than you are. If you are working alone ask someone to read out the instructions to you. Always try out the beginner postures and perfecting them before moving on to more difficult postures. Be always cautious to prevent injury to yourself. It is also advisable to workout in front of a full-length mirror particularly if you are a beginner to check your alignment.

Set aside a minimum of 30 minutes to one hour for a session, although the recommended time to include a variation of postures is generally an hour and a half, which includes time for breathing practices and meditation. If time is short reduce the number of postures and remember NEVER rush through too many.

Some does & Don'ts

- Practice Yoga only after ablution early in the morning on empty stomach
- Bathe before practice.
- Do not wash your body for at least 15 minutes after session
- Use a carpet, mat or blanket for practises
- Dress in comfortable loose-fitting clothes
- Avoid wearing spectacles while practising
- Concentrate on breathing and the limbs or organs being stimulated by the posture
- Start with corpse posture or savasana for the first 3-4 minutes silently offering prayers
- Women should practice postures that are beneficial for regular menstrual cycles
- Pregnant women should do only postures specially suggested for them
- Practise everyday
- Finish Yoga postures with savasana
- After each session spend a few minutes in pranayam and meditation

WARMING-UP

Warming up

A good warm up is absolutely essential in Yoga. The reason behind a decent warm up is mainly to assist you in avoiding injuries and the aches and pains that come with exercise. The physiological reason is to assist your circulatory system in pumping the blood carrying oxygen to your muscles. A warm up can consist of a light walk before exercise and if you have a history of poor circulation, then a warm shower will go a long way in assisting your circulatory system. Once you have activated your system, you can further assist it by doing the following warm up routine, which consist of a few exercises.

Warming up exercises

Given below is recommended warm-up routine before you begin your Yoga sessions.

1. Eye

Keeping your head centred and still, focus your eyes up, down, side to side and diagonally up and down.

Circle your eyes two or three times clockwise, then repeat the action anti-clockwise.

Close your eyes. Rub your hands together and then cup your warmed palms over your eyes. Open your eyes into the darkness and absorb the darkness into your eye sockets for two or three breaths. Close your eyes as you release your hands and then open your eyes, allowing them to come to rest gently on whatever happens to be lying in front of them.

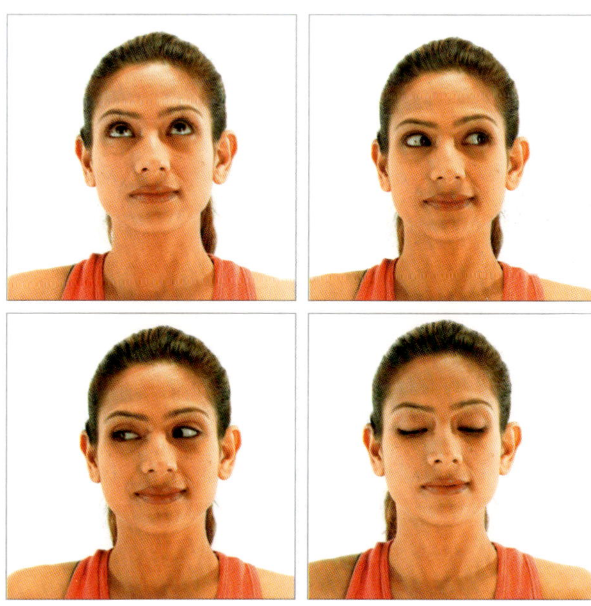

2. Facial Muscles

1.Tighten all your facial muscles, closing your eyes tightly and pursing your lips.

2.Now do the opposite. Open your eyes and mouth as wide as possible and stick out your tongue.

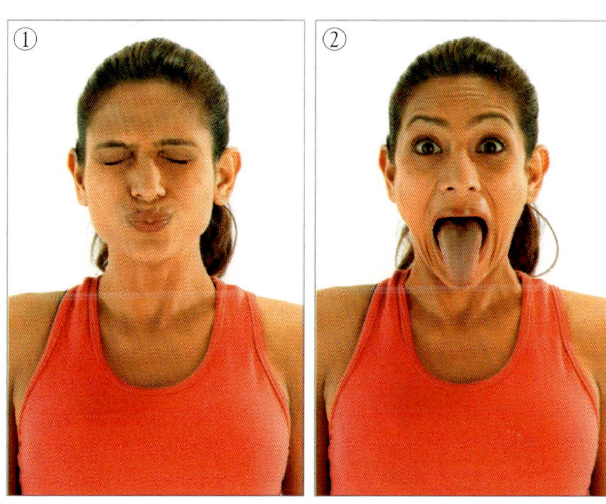

3. Neck warm-ups

Turning the head

Inhaling, turn your head to the right side as far as you can. Exhaling, return your head to the front. Repeat to the left. Alternate the movement two or three times in a flowing manner, keeping your chin parallel to the ground.

Back of the neck

Exhale, then lower your chin down to your chest. Hold for a minimum of two breaths. To recover, inhale, returning your head to the upright position.

Front of the neck

Inhale and raise your chin, stretching the front of your neck. Hold for one or two breaths. Exhaling, lower your chin to your chest and hold for one or two breaths.

4. Circle the waist

Stand with your feet together and your hands on the lower back. Imagine the tailbone dropping down to the ground and the crown of your head extending to the sky. Feel as if you are suspended between sky and earth. Circle your tailbone clock wise for 32 rotations and then reverse, counter clockwise, for 32 rotations. Remember to breathe deeply and regularly, relaxing your belly and jaw and eyes. This will warm up the lower back.

5. Circle the Hips

Stand with your legs apart the width of the hips, feet parallel and toes pointing forward. Place your hands on the outside of the hip socket with your fingers pointing down. Again, suspend the body between heaven and earth, relaxing belly, jaw and eyes. Rotate in an oval 32 times clockwise and 32 times counter-clockwise. This will warm up the hips.

6. Circle the Knees

Stand with your feet together, then bend the knees. Place your hands on the kneecaps with your fingers pointing down. Keep the back extended and the arms straight. Circle the knees clockwise and counter-clockwise, beginning with 6 rotations each direction. As you become used to this exercise, gradually build up to 32 rotations each direction. This warm-up is for the knees and ankles.

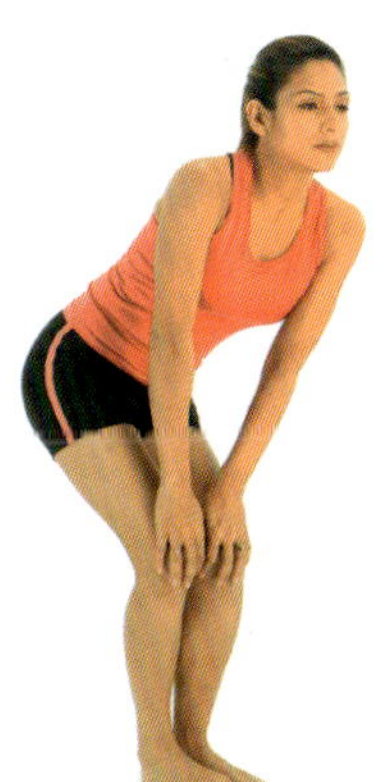

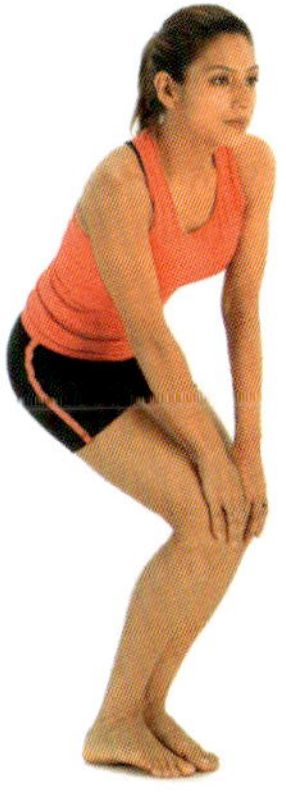

7. Side stretch

Stand with your feet together and stretch your arms overhead. Interlock your fingers and turn the palms to the sky. Press your palms upward and plant the feet firmly downward. As you exhale, stretch to the right, hold the stretch for a few moments, breathing easily. Inhale, coming back to the centre and repeat to the left.

8. Forward Bend

Stand with your feet together parallel and your arms at your sides. Inhale and on the exhale fold forward from the crease of the hips with your hands on the legs above the knee. Lengthen the back. Extend the sides of the torso, lift the belly and ribs up. Do not push back into your knees, but keep the legs straight. Gradually lower the torso down, from the hips, the arms reaching toward the ground. Interlock your fingers and turn the hands over, the palms reaching towards the ground. Do not force this stretch, but let the breath and gravity increase it. Keep your head up. Stay in the stretch for a few normal breaths and come up while inhaling. This warm-up stretches the muscles of the legs and back.

9. Side Chest Stretch

Separate your feet a wide distance, 4 feet or more depending on the length your legs. Point the toes forward. Place your hands above the knees. While exhaling, bend your right knee, keeping the left leg straight. The torso should be in as upright a position as possible. Try not to lean forward. One method of practice is to hold on to a

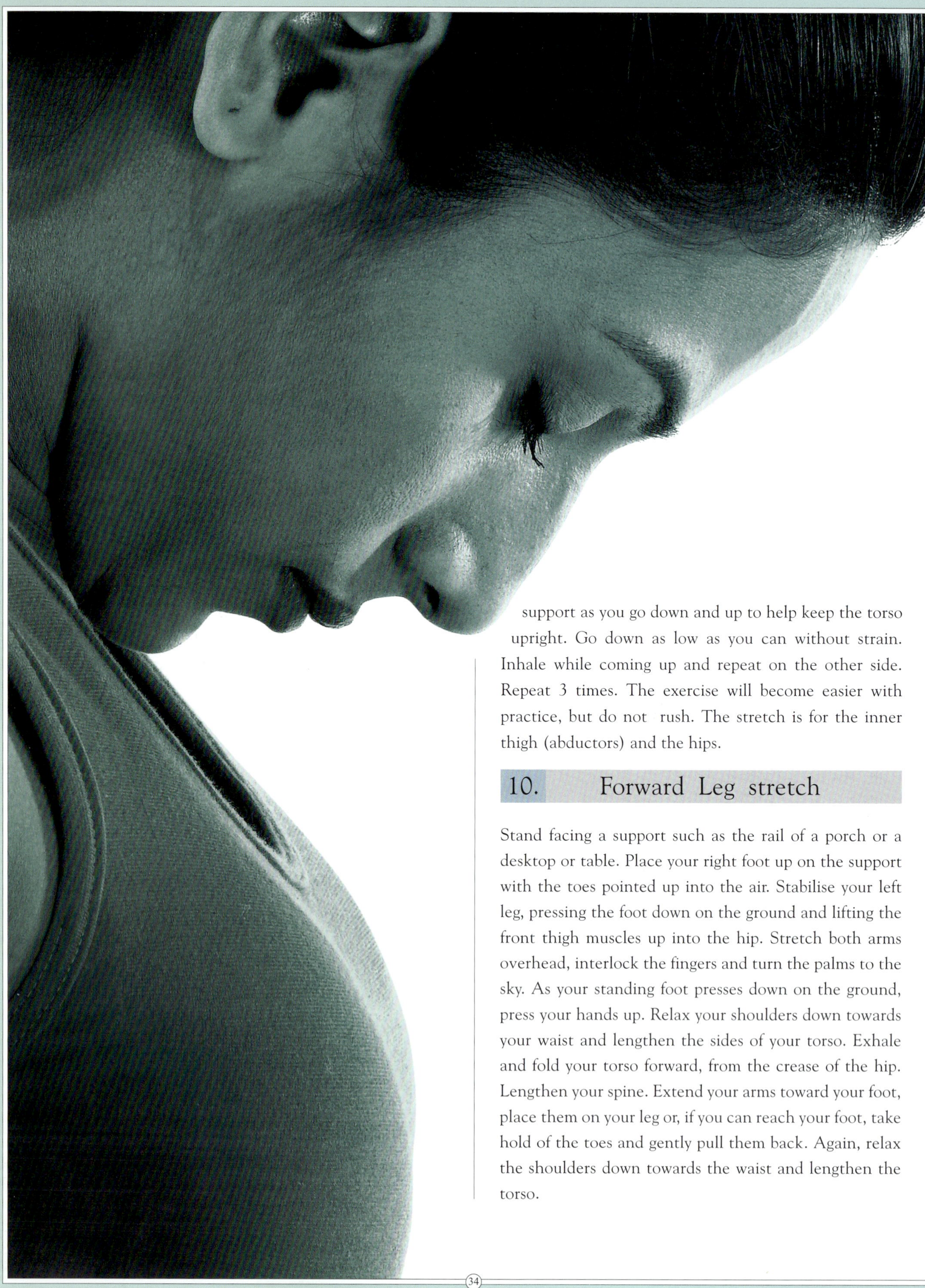

support as you go down and up to help keep the torso upright. Go down as low as you can without strain. Inhale while coming up and repeat on the other side. Repeat 3 times. The exercise will become easier with practice, but do not rush. The stretch is for the inner thigh (abductors) and the hips.

10. Forward Leg stretch

Stand facing a support such as the rail of a porch or a desktop or table. Place your right foot up on the support with the toes pointed up into the air. Stabilise your left leg, pressing the foot down on the ground and lifting the front thigh muscles up into the hip. Stretch both arms overhead, interlock the fingers and turn the palms to the sky. As your standing foot presses down on the ground, press your hands up. Relax your shoulders down towards your waist and lengthen the sides of your torso. Exhale and fold your torso forward, from the crease of the hip. Lengthen your spine. Extend your arms toward your foot, place them on your leg or, if you can reach your foot, take hold of the toes and gently pull them back. Again, relax the shoulders down towards the waist and lengthen the torso.

Reach the chin towards the toes. Do not press into the knees. Make the calf muscle of the extended leg firm and lift the muscles of your upper thigh against your shoulder. This will help stretch the hamstring muscles of the back thigh. Breathe easily. Stay in the stretch until you feel the muscles under the thigh begin to release. This exercise stretches the hamstring muscles, under the thigh, and the calf. Inhale and come up. Do exercise #11 and then repeat #10 and #11 to the left side.

11. Leg stretch & Twist

Keep your right foot up on the support. Your left leg is firm and straight with your foot pressing down into the ground. Place your right hand on the right side of the waist and the left-hand on the right leg. On exhalation, lift the belly and turn the waist to the right. Lengthen the sides of the torso and let the shoulders drop down. Your eye gaze may follow the direction of the turn, but do not twist the neck forcibly. Breathe easily. After you feel the muscles of the side torso begin to release, come slowly back to the original, forward-facing position. This exercise stretches the sides of the torso and releases the hip.

12. Toes to Chin

Stand with your feet together and then turn the left foot outward 45 degrees. Bend your left leg and step your right leg forward, placing the heel on the ground and the toes up. All the weight should be on the left leg. Note that the bent-left knee is over the left foot, not veering in or out of that alignment.

Stretch forward from the crease of the right hip and stretch your hands towards the right foot. You may place your hands on theleg or, if possible, place your hands on the foot, pulling back on the toes and ball of the foot. Keep reaching the chin toward the toes, stretching the spine and torso as well as the legs. Remember not to bend your knees. Do not force this stretch. Breathe easily and let the stretch take place gradually, increasing each day. Inhale as you come up.

13. Swinging Arms

Step into a forward lunge position, with your right leg forward and right knee bending over the foot and your left leg straight. Place your right hand into the lower back on the right side with the fingers pointing downward. Circle your left arm in, brushing the inside of the right knee and continuing up and over the head and around again. Begin by doing eight repetitions and build up to 32. Repeat on the left side. This exercise warms up the shoulder and upper back.

14. Upper-torso Twist

Step into a forward lunge position, with your right leg forward and right knee bent over the foot and your left leg straight. Place your right hand into the lower back on the right side with the fingers pointing downward. Circle your left arm in, brushing the inside of the right knee and continuing up and over the head and around again. Begin by doing eight repetitions and build up to 32. Repeat on the left side. This exercise warms up the shoulder and upper back.

15. Lower-torso Twist

Stand with your feet the width of the shoulders, toes pointed forward and the knees slightly bent. Let your arms dangle relaxed from the shoulders. Breathing easily, twist from the waist, swinging from the right and then left, your hands hitting the outside edge of the hips as you swing. When you are turned to the right your left hand is in front of the torso, the palm slapping the outside of the right hip and your right hand is behind the buttocks slapping the back of the hand to the outside of the left hip. This is reversed as you turn to the left. When you are twisting right your eyes look back to the left inside ankle, and when you twist left they look back towards the right inside ankle. The movement should be relaxed and loose. This movement helps to loosen the middle and lower back.

16. Abdomen Twist

Stand with your feet the width of the shoulders, toes pointed forward and knees slightly bent. Relax your belly. Let your arms dangle from the shoulders in a relaxed manner. Swing to the right and left side, letting your elbows bend so that the back of the left hand hits the right side of your back below your rib cage as you swing to the left and the right palm hits the torso on the left side, and reverse to the right side. Keep your eyes looking forward. Twist from the waist, staying steady with your legs, the knees remaining forward as you turn. This swing is good for the neck and upper back. It is said to bring increased circulation to the area of the kidneys

14. Open Chest Stretch

Stand with your feet the width of the shoulders, toes pointed forward and knees slightly bent. Relax your belly. Let your arms dangle from the shoulders in a relaxed manner. Inhale and lift your arms over your head, palms open to the sky, as the upper back arches and the chest opens. Straighten the legs as you make this arm motion. Exhale and lower your arms in front of the chest down to just below the navel, the palms pressing down to the earth. The knees bend as this motion takes place. Repeat this exercise 8 times. Do the motion slowly and deeply. Feel the air coming into your lungs while inhaling and exhale. Imagine that you are pulling energy into your body from the outside and storing it below your navel and inside.

15. Back to the Square-one

Stand with your feet the width of your shoulders, toes pointed forward and knees slightly bent. Your arms are relaxed at the sides. Again, make sure that your belly is relaxed. Inhale and raise your arms out to the side, palms up at the shoulder level and then above the head in a large circle. Straighten your legs as you make this motion. Exhale and bring your arms down in front of the body, palms down, to the area right below the navel. The knees bend as you make this motion. Repeat this exercise 8 times. Breathe deeply and fully. Imagine that the energy you are a gathering into you is moving through your whole body and then coming back into the area below the navel, where it is stored.

Suryanamaskara or Salutation to the Sun

The Sun Salutation or Surya Namaskar limbers up the whole body in preparation for the yoga Asanas.It is a graceful sequence of twelve yoga positions performed as one continuous exercise. Each position counteracts the one before, stretching the body in a different way and alternately expanding and contracting the chest to regulate the breathing. Practised daily it will great flexibility to your spine and joints and trims your waist.

One round of Sun Salutation consists of two sequences, the first leading with the right foot in positions 4 and 9 (as illustrated), the second leading with the left. Keep your hands in one place from positions 3 to 10 and try to co-ordinate your movements with your breathing. Start by practising four rounds and gradually build up to twelve rounds.

1 Stand erect with feet together and palms in the prayer position in front of your chest. Make sure your weight is evenly distributed. Exhale.

2 Inhaling, stretch your arms up and arch back from the waist, pushing the hips out, legs straight. Relax your neck.

3 Exhaling, fold forward, and press your palms down, fingertips in line with toes - bend your knees if necessary.

4 Inhaling, bring the right (or left) leg back and place the knee on the floor. Arch back and look up, lifting your chin.

5 Retaining the breath, bring the other leg back and support your weight on hands and toes. Keep your head and body in line and look at the floor between your hands.

6 Exhaling, lower your knees, then your chest and then your forehead, keeping your hips up and toes curled under.

7 Seventh post ration in which toes, knees, palms, chest and forhead or chin will be touching on the floor it is called SAshtanga Pranama.

8 Exhaling, curl your toes under, raise your hips and pivot into an inverted "V" shape. Try to push your heels and head down keep your shoulders back.

9 Inhaling, step forward and place the right (or left) foot between your hands. Rest the other knee on the floor and look up, as in position 4.

10 Exhaling, bring the other leg forward and bend down from the waist keeping your palms as in position 3.

11 Inhaling, stretch your arms forward, then up and back over your head and bend back slowly from the waist, as in position 2.

12 Exhaling, gently come back to an upright position and bring your arms down by your side.

The Postures

Simple Postures for the Elderly

It is often found that people over 45-years-of-age especially amongst those who have led a sedentary lifestyle, ailments such as rheumatic pain, arthritis, blood pressure and heart disorders are fairly common. The following Asanas are especially recommended for such people so as to help remove energy blockades in their and joints organs as quickly, efficiently so as to be able to help them do the more regular Yoga Asanas and reap its benefits at the earliest.

These recommended are easy-to-practice and induce a feeling of mental peace and balance thus initiating a sense of harmony with your physical self. These are ideal for revitalising the body and enhancing the functions of the vital organs. Hence these postures are equally good for first time practitioner of Yoga too.

If at anytime while doing these postures should you feel any tiredness or aches rest in a the corpse posture or savasana for a few minutes before continuing.

Anti-Rheumatic Group

The following 10 simple exercises are especially good for people with rheumatic disorders. These are all done in the base posture as detailed below.

Base Posture

Sit with legs stretched forward with palms on either side, with arms held straight. Hold the head up with the neck and spine straight. Close your eyes and relax totally

Toes Bending

Staying in the base posture gently stretch the toes of both feet simultaneously forwards and backwards. Do not move the ankles and stretch the toes gently and in relaxed manner Inhale when stretching the toes backwards and exhale when stretching them forwardRepeat this movement 10 times

Ankle Bending

Remaining in the same posture keep legs slightly apart. Bend the left leg at the knee and pull thighs against your chest.

Swing your leg forward and back holding your position for 3 to 4 seconds Inhale when pulling leg towards you and exhale while pushing leg away from you. Repeat the movements with your right leg.

Ankle Rotation

Staying in the same posture with legs slightly apart and rest heels on the floor Gently rotate the right foot in a clockwise manner at the ankle 10 times Repeat in the anticlockwise manner for another 10 times Do the same with your left foot. Bring both feet together and do the rotation in both directions simultaneously Repeat the movements 10 times in each direction. Keeping the slightly apart but with the big toes touching rotate the ankles in opposite directions Repeat the movements in each direction 10 times. Inhale during the upward movement and exhale on the downward.

Ankle Cranking

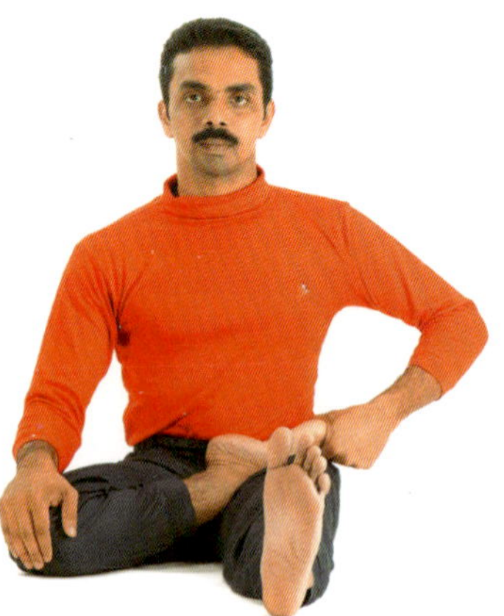

Sitting straight in the base posture gently bend the right-knee and place your leg on your left thigh.

Hold near the right ankle with right hand and hold the right toes with your left. Rotate the right foot 10 times clockwise and 10 times anticlockwise with the left hand.

Repeat the movements with your left leg.

Inhale during the upward movement of the foot and exhale on the downward.

This exercise enhances the blood-flow to the feet and relieves tiredness and cramps.

Knee Bending

Bend your right knee clasping your thighs with your hands.

Raise the leg away from you pulling up the kneecap

Bring your leg down with your heels touching your buttocks and holding thighs close to your chest

Keep head and spine straight and repeat this swinging movement 10 times.

Repeat with your left leg. Inhaling when stretching the leg away and exhale while bending them.

Hip Rotation

Sitting straight in the base posture gently bend the right knee and place your leg on your left thigh.

Hold the right ankle with your left hand

Place palm down on top of the right knee

Rotate the muscles of the thighs with your hands first 10 times clockwise and then anticlockwise

Slowly stretch the knee and repeat with your left leg.

Inhale when raising upwards and exhale while bending forward.

Butterfly Posture

Sitting in the base posture bend legs at the knee bringing the soles of the feet together.

Clasp the feet with both hands and using the elbows for leverage press the legs downwards simultaneously

Bounce the knees up and down permitting the knees to touch the floor without using any undue force.

Do 30 up and down movements.

Placing the palms of your hand on the knees and push the knees to the floor allowing them to spring back. Repeat 20 times, stretch legs and relax. Please Note: People with Sciatica sacral disorders should avoid the butterfly posture.

Wrist rotation

Sit in the cross-legged posture with hands outstretched at shoulder level and palms open straight.

Bend the wrists up pointing the fingers upwards and then bend them down with the fingers pointing to the floor.

Keeping the elbows and fingers straight repeat 10.

Inhale when fingers point upward and exhale when they point down.

Put down your left hand while holding the right in the same position.

Make a fist with your thump inside the palm.

Rotate the wrist 10 times clockwise and 10 times in the anticlockwise direction, keeping fist down.

Repeat with left wrist.

Now rotate both wrists simultaneously first in the clockwise and then the anticlockwise direction.

Practice rotating simultaneously but in opposite directions

10 times at a time.

Inhale when the wrists come up and exhale when they go down.

These exercises are excellent for arthritis and also relieve tension in the wrists due to prolonged writing or keyboard operations.

Shoulder-socket Rotation

Place your right fingers on your right shoulder and your left fingers on your left shoulder with elbows pointing out.

Rotate elbows simultaneously in a large circular motion.

Let the elbows touch on the forward movement and the your palms press against your ears when moving back.

Stretch arms backwards when moving down touching the sides of your body.

Do this movement 10 times first in the clockwise and then in the anticlockwise direction.

Inhale during the upward movement and exhale during the down. This is excellent to relieve strain in shoulder muscles and maintain posture.

Digestive Postures

These following postures are recommended for enhancing the functioning of the digestive system. These are especially good for those who have digestion related disorders such as indigestion, constipation, acidity, flatulence, lack of appetite, including chronic disorders like diabetes and ailments of the reproductive systems and varicose veins.

A short corpse posture or savasana is recommended in-between the practice of these postures till breathing returns to normal. Do not attempt to practice all of these postures one immediately after the other. People suffering from high blood pressure, heart problems, sciatica, slipped disc etc. should not attempt them.

Raised Leg Posture

Lie supine on the floor with palms raise your right leg gently at a 40º angle while inhaling.

Hold the posture for 5 seconds and lower the leg to the floor.

Repeat 5 times and then do the same with the left leg.

Repeat this exercise with both legs simultaneously.

This exercise helps strengthen abdominal muscles, digestive tract muscles, lower back, pelvic and perennial muscles by internal massage of vital organs.

Leg Rotation

Lying supine raise your right leg 5cm off the floor stretching the toes downward.

Rotate the leg clockwise in a circular motion 5 times clockwise and 5 times anticlockwise direction.

Repeat the same with the left leg making sure that your heels remained raised from the floor while rotating the legs.

Now raise both legs together and do the same simultaneously ensuring that your breathing remains normal at all times. While rotating, when the legs move up breath-in and while they move down breath-out. This leg rotation helps hip joints to become more flexible and is recommended for obesity and for exercising abdominal and spinal muscles.

Cycling Posture

Lying supine raise your right leg, bend at the knee bring it back to your chest and then straighten it.

Lower the leg in a forward movement bend, the knee and bring it to the chest again to complete a cycle.

Repeat this 10 times forward and 10 times reverse making sure that your heels do not touch the floor.

Inhale when straightening leg and exhale while bringing it to the chest.

Repeat the same with your left leg Now do the same movement simultaneously with both legs in a cycling manner.

This is very good for the hips and knees and also strengthens abdominal muscles.

Legs-locked Posture or Pavana mukthasana

Lie supine keeping your limbs, torso and head straight.

Bend the right knee and hold it against your chest by interlocking your hands below your knee.

Keeping the left leg straight inhale deeply and on exhalation raise your head and shoulders off the floor.

Try to touch your nose to your knee. Hold your breath for a few seconds counting mentally.

Now inhale slowly while lowering your head and shoulders to the floor.

Exhale and straighten your leg forward before lowering to the floor.

Repeat this 3 times and then do the same with your left leg.

Now bring both your knees together to the chest and repeat the movements 3 more times.

Contra-indications: Individuals suffering from high blood pressure and spinal disorders should refrain from doing this exercise.

Benefits

The benefits of Pavana mukthasana are numerous. It strengthens back muscles, loosens the spinal vertebrae, massages abdominal and digestive organs and eliminates constipation eliminating flatulence accumulated in the abdomen. It massages the pelvic muscles and the reproductive organs often solving disorders of impotence, sterility and menstruation. It is also excellent for people with cardiac disorders, anxiety, back aches, insomnia, headaches, obesity, gout diarrhoea etc.

Universal Spinal Twist

Lie supine with legs together and hands stretched straight down on either side with palms facing down.

Bend the right leg and place it on the on the left knee with your left hand on your right knee.

Gently lower the right knee to the floor and in contact with your left knee.

Gently turn your head to gaze at the middle finger of your right hand.

Make sure that your right hand and shoulders remain on the floor and that your left hand remains on your right knee.

Now turn your head to the left looking at your right knee ensuring that your left leg is straight and relaxed.

Hold this position for 10 second and then return to your original supine position

Repeat these movements with your left leg in the opposite direction.

Make sure you inhale when beginning and exhale when pushing knee to the floor and turning the head.

Breath deeply and rhythmically. Inhale when returning to the supine position and exhale when straightening the leg.

This should ideally be practised soon after forward and backward bending-from-the-hip exercises.

It is excellent for disorders of the hip joint, as well as tightness and tiredness in the lower back.

It also tones your pelvic and abdominal organs.

MEDITATION POSTURES

MEDITATION POSTURES

Sukhasana

Sukhasana is a popular Yoga posture. Sukhasana is a position that helps to concentrate on breathing and the body. Sukhasana also helps strengthen lower back and opens the groin and hips. Sit cross-legged with hands on knees. Then start concentrating on your breath. Remember to keep your spine straight and press on the sit bones down to the ground. Let your knees to lower down slowly. In the case your knees rise above your hips, then sit on a pillow or block. The pillow or the block will support your back and hips. Start taking slow and deep breaths. When you start to inhale the next time, raise your arms above your head. Once you stop inhaling start to exhale and lower down your arms down slowly. Repeat the same process for 5-10 times.

Padmasana or Lotus Posture

This is the completed version of the "Ardha Padmasana."

Sit down stretching legs forward.

Bend the right leg and keep the foot on the left thigh with the sole facing upward.

Ensure that the knees are touching the floor.

Hold the head, neck and spine upright with shoulders relaxed.

Keep hands on the knees in chin/gyan mudra.

Keep the elbows slightly bend.

Keep eyes closed and relax the entire body.

This is a meditative posture hence, spine must remain straight in its final position

One must practise Ardha Padmasana before resorting to practise Padmasana.

Do not forget the limitation.

After keeping one leg on the other thigh, if other leg cannot be placed fully on the other thigh, do not try to put it forcefully.

Those suffering from chronic knee pain, should not practise it.

Those getting cramps in calf-muscles should practise it cautiously.

Ardha Padmasana

Place one foot on the opposite thigh and the other foot on the other thigh. This is known as "Virasana." Since the position of legs is like half of that of Padmasana (i.e. not complete), the posture is called "Ardha Padmasana."

Sit stretching out both legs, hands by the side of the body, palms on the ground, fingers together pointing forward.

Hold the right foot with the left hand and the right ankle with the right hand and place the right leg on the left thigh.

In the same way, place the left leg under the right thigh

Sit erect, place hands on the respective knees. Gaze should be nasal or in front.

While coming back, loosen your hands and stretch out your left leg first.

Then stretch out right leg and return to the original position.

It is considered as a preparatory Asana for Padmasana, therefore, one should practise this Asana first.

While in final position, the knees must touch the ground.

Sidha Yoni Asana

This Asana is meant specifically for women and is a purely meditative Asana.

Sit erect with your legs folded, with one heel pressing the vaginal opening.

The other heel should press the clitoris and pubic bone.

Place the hands on the knees Press the chin against the chest.

Concentrate your gaze towards the centre of your eyebrows.

Keep your head straight without bending with your eyes closed in meditation.

Sit in this position as long as you can and come back to Savasana to relax

This Asana stimulates the sexual organs and controls heart rate and blood pressure.

Sidhasana or Accomplished Posture

Sidhasana is a pure meditative Asana and has innumerable benefits.

Sit erect with your legs folded with one heel pressing the perineum and the other against the pubic bone. In men, one heel should press the area between the scrotum and the anus and the other heel just above the penis. In women, this Asana is called Siddha Yoni Asana and in this position, one heel presses the vaginal opening and the other against the clitoris.

Place the hands on the knees pressing the chin against the chest

Concentrate your gaze towards the centre of your eyebrows.

Keep the head straight without bending with your eyes closed for meditation.

Sit in this position as long as you can and come back to Savasana and relax.

Useful for meditation, concentration, reaching higher state of awareness, purifying body-mind complex, stimulation of all the visceral organs, controlling heart rate, blood pressure and brain wave pattern, regulating emotional and sexual metabolism and increases secretion of testosterone.

VAJRASANA OR THUNDERBOLT POSTURE

The vajra or thunderbolt is regarded as the weapon of lord Indra, the lord of gods. Similarly this Asana may be regarded as the king of all Asanas related with the mind, the king of all the senses. Vajra is major pulse (nadi) directly related with the genito-urinary system, which regulates the sensual energy of body. There are over all fourteen Asanas in Vajrasana series. All these Asanas are related with the digestive system and sensual energy of a person. Therefore control of vajra nadi leads to sublimation and control of sensual energy. Vajrasana series Asanas are most recommended in therapeutic yoga. There is hardly one person who has never been afflicted with sensual or digestive problems. After certain age even waist pain is normal problem. The vajrasana series plays an important role in alleviating waist pain, spinal chord or shoulder pain. These are also quite effective during menstrual disorders and abortions like problems or even normal delivery. That is why these days various doctors recommend yoga for safe and normal delivery. There is no time limits for these Asanas with only provision that you are on empty stomach and healthy. One can perform vajrasana even during menstruation. This relives one from pelvic strain, waist pain or burning sensation. During Vajrasana the vital energy flow is towards sahsradhara from muladhara which helps in meditation. Thus the sensual energy is promoted towards spiritual upliftment. Even persons afflicted with sciatica and slipped-disc who find it unable to sit in meditational postures, can practice vajrasana easily.

③

①

②

- Bend the knees and holding them together sit down.
- Place the buttocks over both the soles.
- Keep the fingers closed.
- Hold the spinal chord and the neck straight.
- Place the palms over the knees.
- Relax and close the eyes.
- Remain conscious towards the physical balance and breathing.
- Do not allow the body to move forward or backward.
- Hold the big toes over each other provided your body is flexible enough.
- Practice this according to one's time and comfort particularly just after the meal.
- During this period breathe from abdomen.

A LYING VAJRASANA

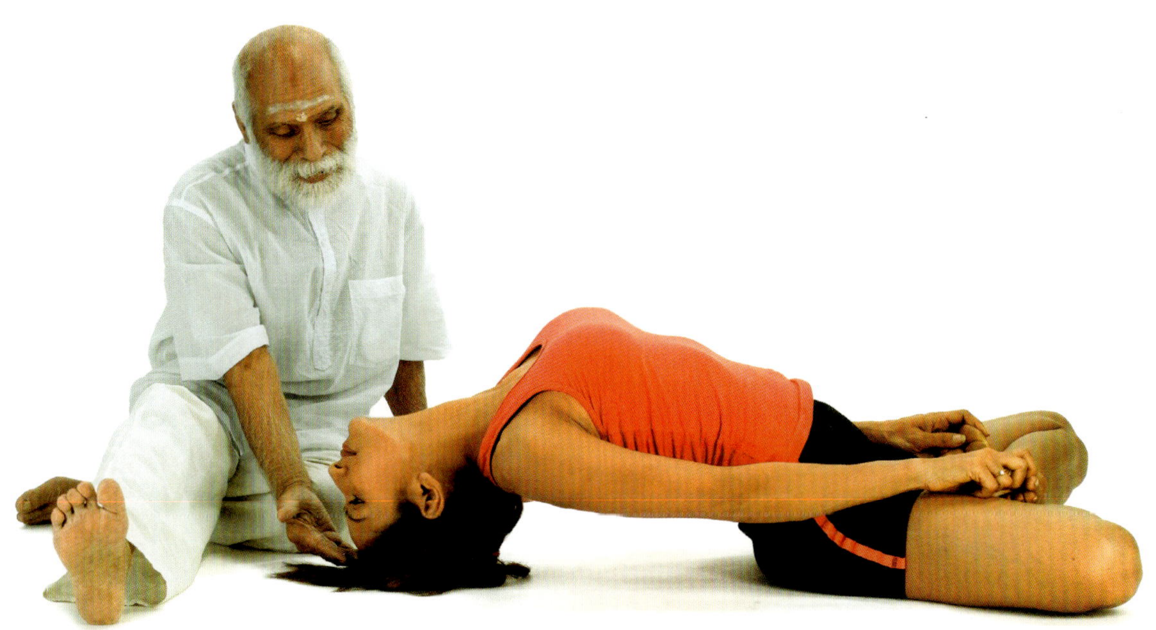

- Sit in the Vajrasana position.
- Thrust the buttocks into the space between the ankles.
- Keep your knees apart and using your elbows to support the body
- Lower the back to the ground.
- You may do this in stages according to your capability.
- After lying down, bring the forearms under the head.
- Once you can do this with ease, the knees may be brought together.
- The abdomen or the chest should not rise from the ground.
- Breathe normally while performing this Asana for about a minute and then slowly revert to the normal position of Vajrasana.
- You may do this Asana at least 8 to 10 times.
- Initially you may practice this Asana with pillow under your knees.

Benefits

- This Asana stretches the rectal muscle of the abdomen.
- Helps in improving digestion by relieving constipation
- Improves flexibility of the knees.
- It helps correct flat feet by encouraging in the development of the arch and instep.
- Beneficial for people with sciatica and hypertension.
- Diabetes can be cured by this posture.

Caution

Do not release the ankles from their position, without raising the back.

People suffering from pain in the hip joint should not attempt this Asana.

AANANDA MADIRASAN OR AN INTOXICATINGLY BLISSFUL POSTURE

- Kneel with thighs and feet together, and slowly sit back on your heels.
- Separate your feet and lower your buttocks between your heels.
- If this is too difficult, put a folded blanket or a bolster under your buttocks.
- Place your palms along the length of your foot.
- Lift your torso, close your eyes, and take deep, relaxing breaths.
- Hold for three to five minutes.
- This posture is not recommended for those with knee problems.

Bhadrasana or Gracious Posture

- Place the two ankles under the scrotum on each side of perineum, the left knee on the left (side) and the right one on right (side) and, firmly holding with the hands the feet which (thus) made to touch the sides, one should remain steady. This is Bhadrasana, that which destroys all diseases.
- Take sitting position stretching both the legs together in front, hands by the side, palms resting on the ground. Fingers should remain together pointing forward.
- Now folding left and right legs slowly at knees join both the soles with each other.
- Hold the legs at ankle by the hands.
- Slowly bring the legs towards yourself till they reach under the perineum.
- Knees should remain on the ground, body erect and gaze in front
- While returning back to the original position loosen the legs and come back to the first position..
- While practising it, a stretch is felt under the thighs therefore practice it carefully.
- Waist and neck should remain erect.
- This is very good posture for lumbar, region and keeps it healthy.

Triyak Bhujangasana Or The Twisting Cobra Posture

Bhujangasana which is mentioned in Surya Namaskar is one of the most important Yoga postures. Bhujangasana is also called by the name of Cobra posture. Bhujangasana helps in stretching the spine, strengthening the back and arms. It also opens the chest and heart.

Start the Asana or the Cobra posture by lying down on your stomach.

Put your legs together and arms at your side palms just under your shoulders.

Inhale and raise your chest and head slowly to the maximum.

While performing the exercise remember to keep your hip muscles tight so that your lower back is not injured. Keep your head up and chest and heart out. Breathe quite a number of times and then relax slowly. After performing the above mentioned steps do the following. Raise yourself on your arms after going as high as possible. At the same time stretch your spine a bit more. But remember; go as far as you are comfortable. While performing the postures keep your pelvis always on the ground. Then breathe several times and come down slowly.

③

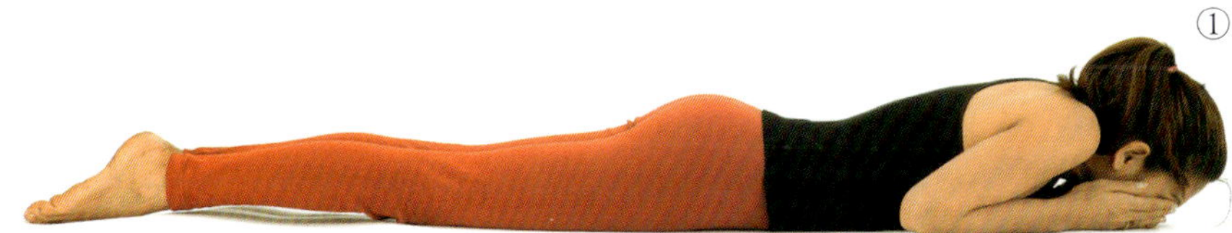

①

Benefits

- Increases flexibility and mobility of the spine and strengthens back muscles.
- Expands the chest and frees the throat area and strengthens and tones abdominal muscles and organs.
- Increases blood circulation to the spine and nerves.
- Alleviates flatulence and helps in digestion.
- Nourishes the pelvic organs with increased blood flow to the region

②

Ustrasana or Camel Posture

- Kneel on the floor, the knees and ankles together, the toes flat on the floor. Bend back and grasp the ankles, the thumbs to the inside of each ankle.
- Push the pelvis forward, throw the head back, and arch the spine strongly.
- Stay in the Posture for ten to twenty seconds, breathing freely.

③

②

①

④

Benefits

- Stretches the spine and feeds the spinal nerves with blood.
- Increases flexibility in the spine and shoulders.
- Improves posture and stretches the abdomen ridding it of fat.
- Expands the chest and corrects rounded shoulders and/or a hunched back.
- Relaxes the neck muscles and opens up the larynges.
- Excellent for persons with respiratory ailments such as asthma and bronchitis.
- Beneficial during pregnancy although caution should be exercised.

Marjasana or the Cat Posture

The Cat Posture teaches you to initiate movement from your centre and to co-ordinate your movement and breath. These are two of the most important themes in Yoga Asana practice. The alignment of your centre depends on the positioning of your pelvis. Therefore, think of your hip positioning as the centre of each Posture. This is important because your spine is the most significant line of energy in every posture and because the way your spine elongates from your centre depends solely on which way your pelvis is turning. If your sacrum is tilted forward (Dog tilt), your spine will project forward before beginning its upward ascent, increasing the curve of your lower back. If your sacrum is tilted backward just like in the Cat tilt, your spine will project backward, rounding your lower back. Every Yoga Posture involves positioning your pelvis in either "cat tilt," "dog tilt," or "neutral"--or in moving toward one of these. In most Yoga Postures, only one of these choices is appropriate.

Start on your hands and knees. Position your hands directly beneath your shoulders and your knees directly beneath the hips. Have your fingers fully spread with the middle fingers pointing straight ahead. Make your back horizontal and flat. Gaze at the floor. This is your "neutral" positioning. When your pelvis is in neutral, your spine will be at full extension, with both the front and backsides equally long.

As you wait for the inner cue, do not sag into your shoulders. Instead, create a line of energy through each arm by pressing downward into your hands and lifting upward out of your shoulders. Go back and forth like this several times to make sure you understand the movement. As you exhale, sag into your shoulders and do the incorrect action; as you inhale, lengthen the arms, lift out of the shoulders and do the correct action.

When you are ready to begin, breathe in deeply. As you exhale, turn your hips into "Cat Tilt". Do this by gently pulling the abdominal muscles backward toward the spine, tucking the tailbone (coccyx) down and under, and gently contracting the buttocks. Press firmly downward with your hands in order to stay lifted out of the shoulders, and press the middle of your back toward the ceiling, rounding your spine upward. Curl your head inward. Gaze at the floor between your knees.

③

As you inhale, turn your hips into "Dog Tilt". Do this by releasing the grip of the buttocks, reversing the tilt of your pelvis, and curving your spine into a smoothly arched backbend. The pubic bone will move backward through the legs, the sitting bones will turn upward, and the sacrum will change its angle.

Keep the navel backward toward the spine as you do this, and continue pressing downward into your hands to lengthen the arms and stay lifted out of the shoulders. Lift your chest away from the waist, lift your head, slide the shoulder blades down your back, and either gaze at a point on the floor in front of you or upward toward the ceiling - or close your eyes and immerse yourself in the way this feels.

Feel the flow of the curve. Increase the curve by tilting your pelvis more and moving the spine deeper into your back, bringing the curve up your back. Do this without sagging into the shoulders. Arch the full length of your spine to its maximum.

①

②

Benefits

- The Cat Posture loosens your back and spine
- It stretches the front and back of your body and frees your neck and shoulders.
- Doing the Cat Tilt elongates your back muscles and makes your abdominal muscles contract.
- The Dog Tilt makes your back muscles contract as the abdominal muscles stretches.
- Doing these postures stimulate the spinal fluid and the digestive tract.
- It improves circulation through the spine and is excellent for respiratory disorders.
- It is also beneficial in managing stress and is very beneficial during pregnancy.

Caution

- Keep shoulders down and your neck extended.
- Place a folded Yoga Blanket under your knees to protect you from pressure or pain.
- Be extremely careful should you be suffering from chronic or recent back pain or injury.

Kati Chakrasana or Waist Rotating Posture

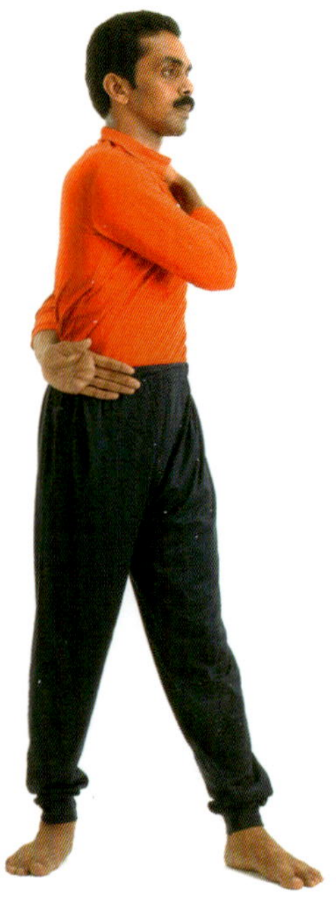

Stand with feet shoulder width apart. Inhale as you raise your arms level to shoulders (a). Keeping the feet flat on the floor, exhale as you twist the upper body to the right side, wrapping the right arm behind the waist and the left hand onto the right shoulder. Turn the head fully to the right to look behind (b). Inhale back to the centre position as in (a). Exhale as you twist to the opposite side (c). Return to the centre position (a). Do 7 more twists to each side, flinging the arm loosely and fast from side to side. All 8 rounds should take no more than 30 seconds.

Salabhasana or Grasshopper Posture

Unlike most Yoga Asanas, the Salabhasana requires a sudden movement to get into the posture. Its effects supplement those of the Cobra. However this posture concentrates on the lower half of the body. To begin with, you may only manage to raise your legs a few inches off the floor - in fact, it is at this stage that this posture resembles a Locust, tall in air. With regular practice you will discover how to contract your lower back muscles to thrust your legs up high, as well as developing the necessary strength. In time, your legs will come to extend beyond your head as in the photograph.

③

Lying on your front, inhale and roll on to your side. Make two fists and place them side-by-side, with thumbs pressing into your thighs. Bring your elbows as close together as possible.

Benefits

- It strengthens the abdomen, lower back and legs.
- Like the other backward bends, it massages the internal organs.
- Ensures efficient functioning of the digestive system and prevents constipation.
- Excellent for the nervous system including the solar plexus and the entire abdominal area.
- Tone leg muscles and strengthens the shoulders.
- Increases blood flow to the head and neck nourishes facial tissue and the brain.
- Beneficial for the bladder and the prostrate gland.

①

②

Matsyasana or The Fish Posture.

③

Sit in Padmasanana.

Slowly take the help of your elbows to lie down on your back.

Slowly lie on your back completely. Now with the help of elbows or palms bend your head backward and place middle of the head on the ground.

Catch hold of the toes with your index fingers and place the elbows on the ground.

While returning to original position, release the toes and taking the help of your hands straighten your head.

Now taking the help of elbow sit in padmasana.

Do not bend your neck backward with a jerk.

While bending neck backward, the spine will be arched maximum.

While returning you can release your legs in sitting position or even in lying position.

①

②

Benefits

- Expands the chest and allows for deeper breathing.
- Excellent for the thyroid and parathyroid glands that regulate body metabolism.
- Strengthens the back and nourishes spinal nerves.
- Alleviates tension in the upper back and increases mobility in the pelvic area.
- Facilitates easy digestion and elimination.
- Recommended for menstrual disorders.
- Offers relief from asthma, bronchitis, backache and cervical spondylosis.

Ardha Matsyendrasana or Half Spinal twist by sitting

Sit stretching the legs straight forward.

Bending the right leg plant its foot on the floor, toes forward, left side of the left knee.

Bend the left leg, keep its sole around the right buttock contacting its foreleg on the floor and pass the left arm between the chest and the right knee.

Keeping the right knee and its foreleg out hold the right ankle or its big toe with the left hand. The right knee should be just close and out of the left armpit. Sit straight.

Raise the right arm front at the shoulder level and gaze at its finger tips. Simultaneously twist to the right moving the right arm, torso and head as far as possible using the left arm as lever against the right leg, without using the back muscle.

Look over the right shoulder and place the right arm bending its elbow and wrapping the left side around the wrist or bending the right elbow place its fore arm as high as possible pointing its fingers up between the shoulder blades. It enforces the straightness of the spine. Hold this final pose one to two minutes.

Breathing: Inhale during forward position. Exhale while twisting the body. Breathe slowly and deeply during the final pose. Practice it after some forward and backward bending poses.

Caution

- Women after 2 or 3 months pregnancy should not practice it. Patients suffering from peptic ulcer, hernia and hyperthyroidism should avoid it. Though it helps to cure sciatica and slipped disc diseases, great care should be taken.

③

Benefits

- It tones the spine nerves and back muscles. It relives lumbago muscular spasm. It alleviates indigestion. It regulates adrenal secretion and bile. It also cures Sinusitis, hay fever, bronchitis, Constipation, Colitis, menstrual disorders, Urinary tract and Spondylitis.

①

②

"Yoga is the stilling of the restlessness of the mind."

-YOGA SUTRAS

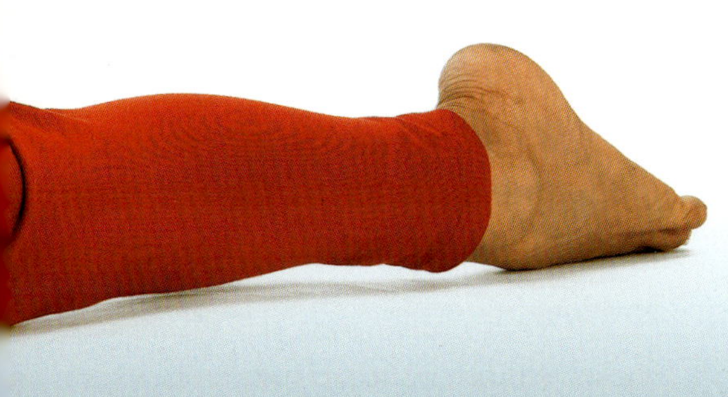

Paripurna Naukasana or The Boat Posture

Paripurna Naukasana is a compound word that translates to mean "a complete boat." This is in reference to the resemblance of the balanced posture to that of a boat. There are two variation to this Asana namely Ardha Naukasana and Ubhaya Padangusthasana.

- Sit with legs together, the knees bent and the soles of the feet firmly on the ground.
- Extend the arms straight in front and parallel to the floor with fingers pointing forward.
- Lean back by raising your legs off the ground and balancing your weight and extent your feet.
- Keep the spine straight and make sure your head and neck are aligned with your spine.
- Raise your legs at a 45-degree angle off the ground so that your torso resembles the alphabet 'V'.
- Hold this position for 3 to 8 breaths.

Ardha Chandrasana or The Crescent Moon Posture

- This posture is usually done as a prelude to Hanumanasana or the splits.
- Kneel on all fours with toes pointing out behind you.
- Bring the right leg forward and place your foot on the floor with toes pointing straight so that your foot are at right angle to your knee.
- Move toward your left hip and stretch across the front of your left hip placing your hands on either sides of your right foot.
- Gently bring your torso upright position and bring your hands together in the prayer posture.
- Keep your shoulders pressed down and more your head forward so as to stretch your spine.
- Look straight ahead and hold this position for 4 to 8 breaths and then reverse the posture to come to position number one.
- Repeat with your left leg and after both sides evenly rest for a few minutes to restore your body symmetry.

Dhanasuran or The Bow Posture

The bow or dhanurasana posture raises both halves of the body at once, combining the movements of the cobra and grasshopper and countering the plough and the forward bend. Like an archer stringing a bow, you use your hands and arms to pull your trunk and legs up together to form a curve. This tones your back muscles and maintains the elasticity of your spine, improves posture and increasing vitality. Balancing the weight of the body on your abdomen also reduces abdominal fat and keeps the digestive and reproductive systems healthy. The rocking bow yoga posture, in particular, gives your internal organs a powerful massage. Initially, you will find it easier to lift your knees with legs apart; more advanced students should aim to perform the bow pose keeping legs together.

③

Lie down on your front, head down. Inhale and bend your knees up, then reach back with your hands and clasp your ankles. Exhale.Inhaling, raise your head and chest and, simultaneously pull your ankles up, lifting the knees and thighs off the floor. Arch backward and look up. Take three deep breaths in this Yoga Posture, then exhale and release it. Come into the Bow, then rock forward as you exhale, backward as you inhale. (Don't use your head to rock.) Repeat up to ten times, then relax.

②

Benefits

①

- Makes the entire spinal column more flexible.
- Corrects unnatural curvature of the spine if any.
- Stretches, tones and massages the abdominal muscles.
- Reduces accumulation of fat in the abdominal area.
- Opens the solar plexus and expands the chest.
- Improves digestion and increases blood flow to the abdominal organs.
- Revitalises the kidneys and adrenal glands.
- Soothes the nervous system.

Gomukhasana

- Sit in Gomukhasana (simply arranging the legs only).
- Now fold your right hand at the elbow and take it towards back.
- Place the back part of the palm on your back. Palm should remain in between the two shoulders. Elbow will point towards the ground.
- Fold your left hand at the elbow and bring it to the back from above the shoulder. Elbow should point towards the sky.
- Now hold fingers of right hand from the fingers of left hand. This is called Baddhahasta Gornukhasana
- Now, release your hands, stretch out your legs.
- Then again practise it from the other arrangement of the legs and hands.

Please Note: If hands could not catch each other then keep them only folded towards back.

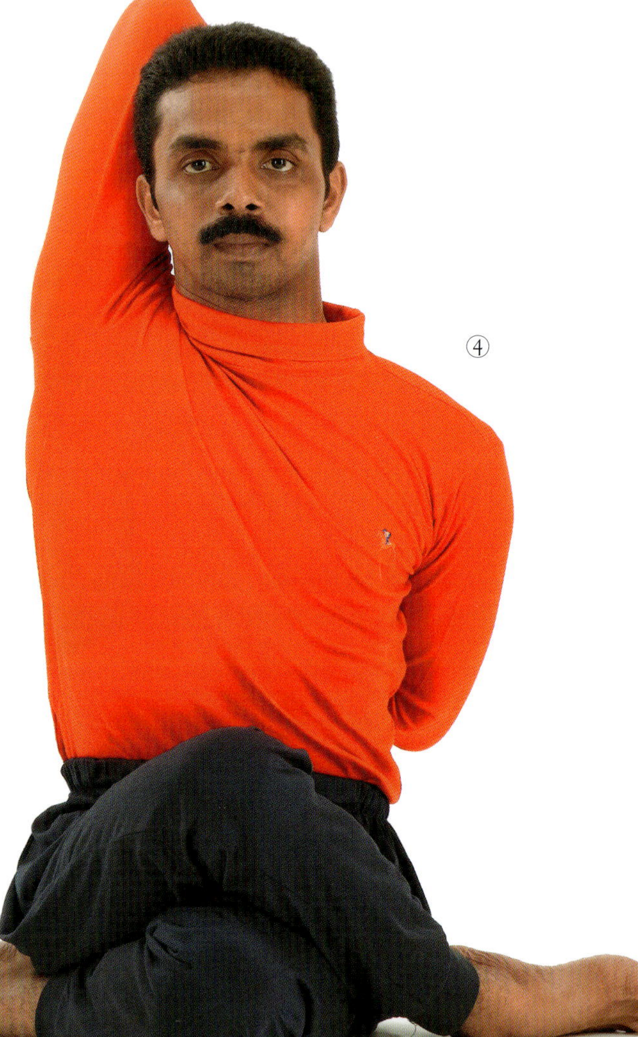

④

Benefits

- Its benefits and limitations are same as in Gornukhasana.
- This strengthens the muscle of the back and biceps.

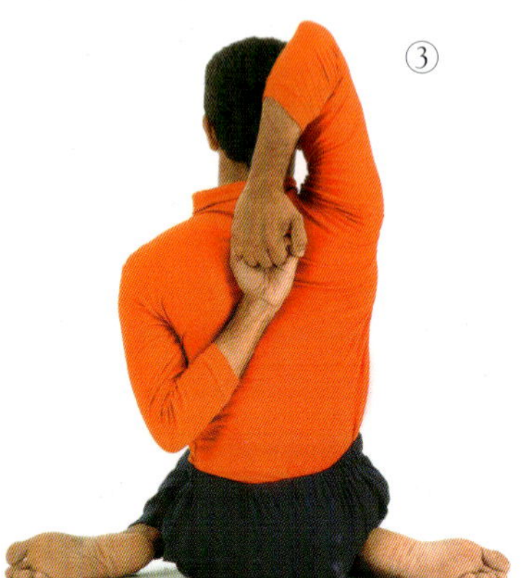

③

②

①

STANDING POSTURES

Tadasana

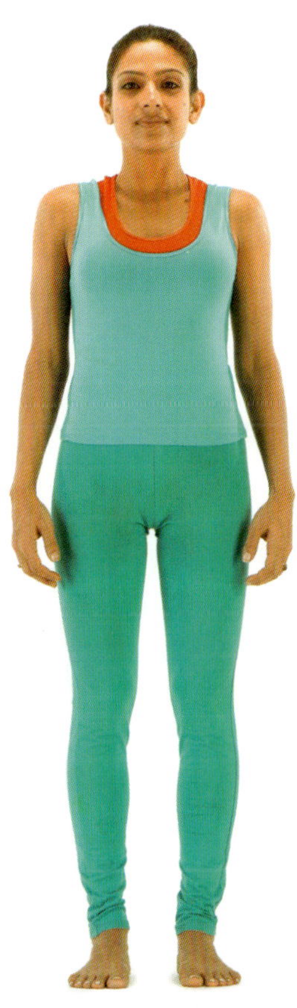

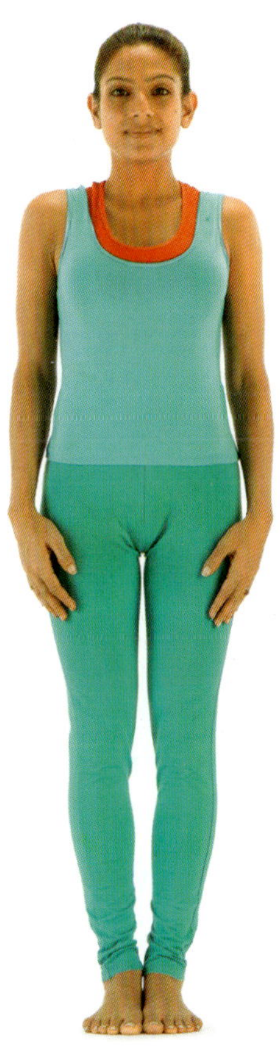

Tadasana posture helps in improving body posture, balance and self-awareness. Tadasana is a deceptive posture as it looks simple to perform.

Stand with your feet together, hands at your sides and eyes looking forward.

Raise your toes and then place them back down on the ground.

Slant the pubic bone a little forward. Lift your chest up and out in moderation.

Raise the head up and lengthen the neck by lifting the base of your skull upwards.

Press on into the ground with your feet and lift your legs First the calves followed by your thighs.

Start breathing and remain in the same posture and stay calm.

While you inhale feel as if the breath is coming up through the floor, rising through your legs, trunk up into your head. When you start exhaling watch your breath as it passes down from your head through the chest and stomach, legs and finally feet. Pause for some breaths; relax and repeat the same process. When you are performing the next inhaling exercise, raise your arms over your head and again pause for some breaths. Then put down your arms on exhale. Remember to warm yourself up by creating rhythm between raising and lowering of arms along with your breath. This part is very crucial in the performance of Tadasana.

A moment's contact with a saintly person becomes
a boat to cross the vast mundane ocean of life

Trikonasana or Triangle Posture

- Inhale and stand erect keeping feet 1-metre apart.
- Exhale and turn right foot to the right.
- Inhale & stretch arms sideways to shoulder level.
- Exhale and body to the right bending the knee slightly.
- Inhale, keep the right palm on the right foot keeping arms in a straight line.
- Exhale turn palms forward.
- Inhale looking at the left thump.
- Retain for 10-15 seconds rhythmically breathing.
- Return to the starting posture in the reverse order.
- Now do the opposite side.
- Inhale raising the arms; exhale when bending and retain breath in the final posture.
- Inhale raising the torso.

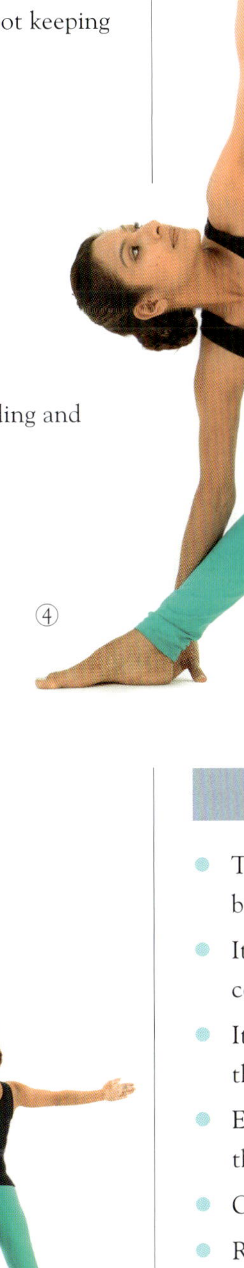

④

③

① ②

Benefits

- This posture is excellent for general well being of the entire body.
- It stimulates appetite, alleviates constipation and strengthens the pelvic region.
- It stimulates and tones the sexual organs as well as the leg muscles.
- Expands the ribcage and tones the nerves around the spinal column.
- Gently massages the liver and the spleen
- Recommended for pregnant women during the first 3 months of pregnancy.

Utthita Janu Sirasana or Head between knees pose by standing

It is Similar to Paschimottanasana by sitting. Stand erect raising both the hands straight to the sky. Bend the trunk of the body and the arms to form a straight line paralled to the floor, keeping the legs straight perpendicular to the floor.

Again bend the body down and plant the palms on the floor touching outer sides of both feet.

Bend the head so that the forehead may touch the knees, keeping the legs straight, don't bend the knees.

Bring both the hands back through both outer sides of the foreleg and hold the wrist each other.

Variation: 1. Stand keeping the feet about half a meter apart, arms besides the body and head facing forward. Raise the arms in front at the chest level.

Bend forward from the hips take the arms around the out side of the legs.

Grasp one wrist or claps the hands bending the calves.

Keeping the legs straight, without strain bring the head towards the knees by slightly bending the elbows and using the strength of the arm muscles. In the final pose the trunk rests against the thighs and the wrists or elbows are held behind the claves or lower legs. Hold this final position comfortably for some time.

① ②

Release the hands and raise the trunk slowly to the upright position. Stretching the arms out in front of the chest, lower the arms to the starting position. Repeat up to 5 rounds.

Variation 2: Stand as in variation 1 bending from the hips and wrapping the arms around the back of the knees. Keep the arms horizontal with elbows pointing out to the sides.

Keeping the legs bent bring the hands forward in between the legs and firmly interlock the fingers behind the back of the neck. Relax the back muscles. Slowly straighten the legs, but the fingers should not slip from behind the neck. In the final position the head will face backward.

④

Breathing: Inhale while raising the arms; Exhale fully before bending. Retain the breath outside while bending forward and holding the final position, while returning to upright position inhale. Exhale during lowering the arms.

Benefits

It stimulates Pancreas, relax the hip joints and hamstring muscles, massages the spinal nerves, and revitalizes the brain by supplying blood flow to that area.

③

Parswa uthana Janu Shirasana or Knee to head pose to the Side by standing.

Stand keeping the feet up to meter apart according to the height, toes forward, facing straight toward the front leg, hanging the arms sideways. Turn your trunk and head just in front keeping the palms on either side of the thighs. Turn again the trunk and head to the starting pose joining the palms together and keeping the fingers upward. Let the palms rest on the back of the waist. Bend the trunk and head backward. Let the trunk and head bend forward from the hip. The trunk should be parallel to the floor. Again bend the trunk and head so that the forehead may touch on the knee of the leg kept forward. Slowly move the elbow joints and folded palms upward to the middle of the back.

Benefits: It stimulates pancreas, improves the digestive power, massages both sides of the spinal nerves, improve the blood flow to the brain.

⑦

①

②

③

④

⑤

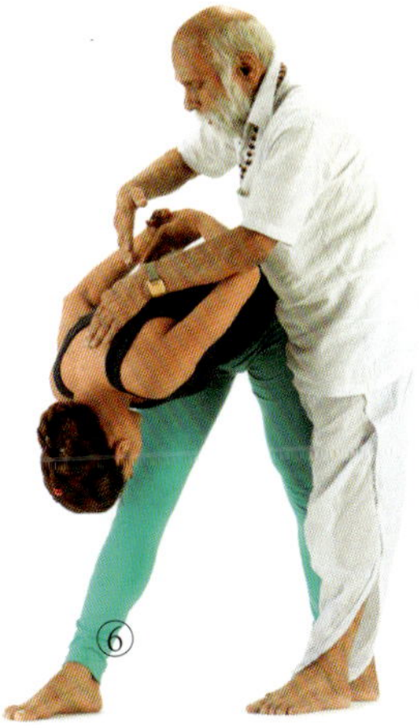

⑥

Service divided by ego is devotion.
When the ego will be Zero, devotion will be infinitive.

Sarvangasana or Shoulder-stand

Sarvangasana is an important Yoga posture that helps in proper thyroid function and strengthening of abdomen. Sarvangasana also stretches upper back, improves blood circulation and encourages relaxation. Doing Sarvangasana is pretty simple and easy

- Lie on your back and lift your legs up.
- Place your hands on your lower back for support, resting your elbows and keeping upper arms on the ground.
- Make sure the weight is on your shoulders and mid to upper back and not your neck. Start breathing deeply and remain in the same posture for at least up to 5-10 breaths.
- To come to the normal position keep your legs straight and lower them down slowly and gradually.
- This part helps in the exercise of your abdominal muscles as well.

③

①

②

④

Sirsasana or Head-stand Posture

Sirsasana is the posture in which the navel is above and the palate below, the Sun above and the Moon below is known as Viparitakarani or topsy-turvy posture. On the first day one should remain for a very short time with one's head below and feet above. The duration of this practice should be gradually increased day by day.

1. Sit on soles. place knees on the ground.
2. Frame finger lock with both hands.
3. Making a triangle from finger-lock and elbows, place it on ground.
4. Bending forward, place middle of the head on the ground near finger-lock.
5. Now straighten your legs.
6. Slowly bring the toes to your neck raising the buttocks up.
7. Soles will automatically leave the ground by practise. The thighs and knees will touch the abdomen.
8. By balancing raise your legs from thigh-joint, knees will remain folded.
9. Now raise the knees also and completely balance your body on head with the support of the elbows.
10. While returning to the original position fold your knee first. Then fold your legs from thigh and let the thigh and knee touch your abdomen.
11. Now slowly place the soles on the ground. Slowly raise your head also and sit on soles.

Things to Remember

While practising Sirsasana, place that part of your head on the ground on which the spine can remain erect

Do not raise your legs with jerk. Slow and gradual practice will "raise your legs up automatically.

In the beginning practise it under the guidance of a teacher because there is a fear of falling down.

While returning, do not raise your head soon after completing Asana. There remains a fear of getting giddiness. Therefore, keep your head near finger-lock for some time and then raise the body.

Benefits and Limitations

1. This increases the blood circulation in head and memory power is improved
2. This strengthens the nervous-centres of the whole body and maintains the health of endocrine gland.
3. Digestive system is also benefited through this Asana.
4. According to Swami Kuvalayanandaji it is beneficial against congested throat, diseases of liver and spleen and in Visceroptosis.
5. Those suffering from high blood pressure or heart disease should not practise it.
6. Those having cough or chronic cold also should not practise it.

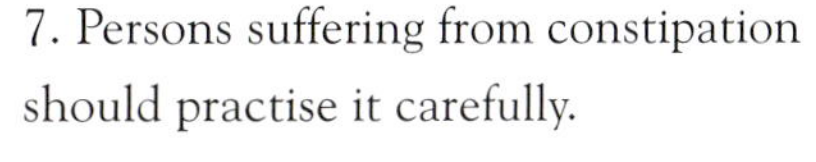

7. Persons suffering from constipation should practise it carefully.

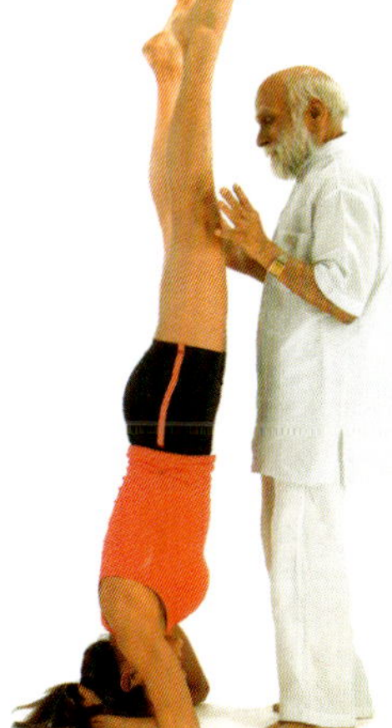

Halasana or Plough Posture

④

- Lie flat on your back with legs and feet together.
- Arms at the sides, closed and placed beside the thighs.
- Keeping your legs straight, inhale slowly.
- Raise your legs to 30, 60 and 90, pausing at each stage.
- Exhale and push your legs further over and above the head.
- Let the toes touch the floor without bending your knees.
- Stretch your legs so that your chin presses tightly against the chest.
- Raise your hands and try to hold the toes.
- Retain the posture from 10 seconds to as long as possible while breathing normally.
- Exhale and return to starting position.
- Slowly go through the process in the reverse order up to the starting pose.
- Hernia, high blood pressure, ulcer, heart, backache and cervical spondylosis patients should avoid this Asana.
- This Asana improves digestion and strengthens the spine. It helps in asthma, diabetes, menstrual disorder and constipation. To be avoided by women during menstruation and pregnancy.

①

②

③

RELAXATION POSTURES

"The soul that moves in the world of the senses and yet keeps the senses in harmony... finds rest in quietness."
The Bhagavad Gita

Makarasana or the Crocodile Posture

- Lay down on the stomach and while exhaling stretch your legs
- Keeping the feet apart, toes turned out and with ankles resting on the mat.
- Rest your chin rest on your cupped palms with elbows resting on the mat.
- Elbows should not be placed too far apart as this can cause undue strain.
- Ensure that your spine is relaxed and breathe deeply and rhythmically.
- Makarasana is yet another important relaxation posture.
- Keep arms on the floor and rest the side of your head on them.
- Inhale from the coccyx to the neck and exhale from the neck to the coccyx.
- Excellent for those suffering from spinal disc disorders and helps restore normalcy for the spinal column.
- It is also recommended for the cure of asthma and other ailments of the lungs

Kundalini energy sleeps on the coccyx for liberating the Yogis and for binding the fools in the mundane world. He who knows it knows Yoga.

Matsya-Kridasana or the Flapping fish Posture

- Lying on the right side of the abdomen keep your fingers interlocked under the head and breath out.
- Bend your left leg sideways bringing the knee close to the rib cage while breathing in.
- Keep the right leg straight and swivel your arms to your left. Rest the right side of the head in the crook of the right arm.
- Be totally relaxed breathing normally and then change sides.
- This posture is excellent for stimulating digestion, relief from sciatica, slipped disc and backache.
- Matsya-Kridasana is ideally suited for women in their latter stages of pregnancy between the 4th and 6th month.
- It is also beneficial in distributing excess weight if any around the waist.

Simhasana or Lion Posture

- In this the body resembles a lion, with claws drawn, tongue hanging out and eyes cantered in the middle of the eyebrows.
- Sit down keeping the right foot below the scrotum and under the left buttock.
- Place the left foot under the right buttock. The right ankle should be over the left one.
- The knees are to be kept 45cms apart and touching the floor.
- Let the body weight fall on the thighs and knees.
- Lean forward with buttocks slightly raised
- Place hands on your knees with the fingers spread out.
- The torso and spine should be kept straight.
- Gaze at the tip of the nose and open the mouth wide
- Protrude the tongue out and roar like a lion.
- Do this 10 to 15 times
- Tonsillitis and other throat diseases in the initial stages are cured.
- The neck muscles are also toned.

"That food which is stale, tasteless, putrid, rotten, and impure refuse, is the food liked by the tamasic." - BHAGAVAD GITA, 17-10

Savasana or the Corpse Posture

Savasana is yet another vital Yogic posture. Savasana relaxes and invigorates your body and mind. It also relieves pressure, anxiety and calms the mind. Probably the most important posture, the Corpse, also known as savasana, is as simple as Tadasana (the Mountain posture). Savasana is generally performed at the end of a session aiming at relaxation. The "conscious" part of Savasana is the most difficult because people tend to drift off to sleep while doing Savasana. Start b+y lying on your back and keep your feet somewhat apart; keep arms at your side with the palms facing up. Then close your eyes and take several deep breaths. Allow your body to sink into the ground. Aim at a specific part of your body to feel relaxed. For example, when starting with feet, you have to imagine that the muscles and skin are slowly relaxing. In the process you feel like letting these parts melting into the ground. After performing on your feet you can move to other body parts like calves, thighs face and head. At the end, breathe in a relaxed mode and remain in the same posture for a few minutes